When in Doubt, HUG 'EM!
*How to Develop a Caring Church*

HOW TO DEVELOP a CARING CHURCH

# when in doubt, HUG 'EM!

CECIL B. MURPHEY

JOHN KNOX PRESS
ATLANTA

The Scripture quotations in this publication are from the Revised Standard Version Bible, copyright 1946, 1952, and © 1971 by the Division of Christian Education, National Council of the Churches of Christ in the U.S.A. and used by permission.

Chapter 9 was previously published in a modified form in *Christianity Today,* copyright © 1977, and is used by permission.

"Fill My Cup, Lord" is from Richard Blanchard, *Dove Songbook,* Hope Publishing Company, © 1975.

Library of Congress Cataloging in Publication Data

Murphey, Cecil B
  When in doubt, hug 'em!

  1. Pastoral theology.  I.  Title.
BV4011.M84      253      77–15751
ISBN 0-8042-1890-0

Copyright © 1978 John Knox Press
Printed in the United States of America

## contents

|     | Introduction                       | 7   |
|-----|------------------------------------|-----|
| 1.  | Experiencing a Difference or, A Congregation in Action | 9   |
| 2.  | Do You See What I See?             | 14  |
| 3.  | It's Only a Name                   | 21  |
| 4.  | A Visitor Comes Only Once          | 27  |
| 5.  | It Starts With Me                  | 34  |
| 6.  | Lots of Love to Share              | 42  |
| 7.  | When *We* Pray                     | 50  |
| 8.  | Where-Are-You? Time                | 56  |
| 9.  | They Count, Too                    | 65  |
| 10. | Measuring Up                       | 71  |
| 11. | But Not for Everyone               | 77  |
| 12. | Caring Means *Doing*               | 83  |
| 13. | After They Join                    | 89  |
| 14. | When in Doubt, Hug 'Em             | 95  |
| 15. | Pastors Need People, Too           | 101 |
| 16. | I'm Single and Alone               | 109 |
| 17. | Sharing Grief                      | 116 |
| 18. | Caring Through Fun and Fellowship  | 121 |
| 19. | And a Few Other Things, Too        | 128 |
| 20. | My Motives Are Showing             | 136 |
|     | P.S.                               | 143 |

*for*
*my caring supporting hugging friends*
*at Riverdale Presbyterian Church*
*and for*
*Dick Ray, Charlie Shedd, Gary Sledge*
*and Don Tinder*
*because you cared enough to encourage me.*

*And special thanks*
*to Vicki Nichols whose ministry at the*
*IBM typewriter in typing the final*
*draft is another example of caring*
*in our church.*

# introduction

Della arrived early for Sunday school. I had turned on the air conditioner in a classroom and saw her come in. She stopped, barely inside, leaned her head against the jamb, and closed her eyes.

"Anything wrong?" I asked.

"Oh, no," she said softly and then laughed nervously. It's only—well—maybe you think I'm silly, but I do this every week. I pause here for a few seconds. I feel at peace. Life isn't bad for me at home, nothing like that. It's only that I sense this is a special place. Like—like Noah's ark."

She laughed self-consciously and said, "Maybe that sounds like I've been teaching first-graders too long. But I think of this as the animals might have thought when they went inside Noah's ark. They were safe. Nothing to worry about. That's a little of how I feel when I come to church. In a couple of hours I'll be out there struggling with the rest of the world. But it's this time here every week that gives me strength to keep on."

I liked that. Della's statement fits in with my philosophy about the church and its role. No one needs to tell us about our isolated, impersonal world. We experience it. We feel it. But I believe the church ought to provide the kind of place where people are affirmed, where they leave feeling better, happier, healthier, and more equipped to cope with life.

I see the church of Jesus Christ as the primary place for caring to take place—people *actively* caring about people.

# 1.
## experiencing a difference, or, a congregation in action

One summer we spent our vacation in the Atlanta area where I am a pastor. When Sunday rolled around we decided to visit Phil's church. We'd known Phil a couple of years and liked him and had wanted to hear him preach.

As we arrived, an usher nodded to us, thrust a bulletin in my hand, and walked toward the other side of the foyer. We moved inside the sanctuary and sat down. During the announcement time, Phil said, "And my good friends, Cec and Shirley Murphey are visiting with us today. We're glad to have you both."

We smiled back. We were the only ones of the 118 people present that morning introduced as visitors.

When the service ended, we headed up the aisle. No one spoke to us. No one shook hands. No one said, "We're glad you're visiting with us today." People scurried out the front door and toward the parking lot.

Phil shook our hands, mumbled something about how glad he was to see us again and that we'd have to get together again soon.

By the time we reached the parking lot, we noticed that almost all the cars had zipped out. Several lined up in the drive and only two cars remained in the lot as we drove out.

Driving away from the church, Shirley said, "Not very friendly, are they?" I shook my head. Not even after we had been introduced as visitors. Still not a single person acknowledged our presence.

Perhaps you've had a similar experience. It's like walking out of a concert hall. A vast foyer filled with strangers going separate ways. No common interests. No one speaks to you. Each group rushes for the parking lot.

But in the church? Surely that ought to be different. The place of the "fellowship of the saints." Not people who come in as strangers and go out the same way! Not from people who have a real relationship with Jesus Christ and are bonded by a living fellowship.

But it happens, doesn't it?

In contrast, Becky left Riverdale Presbyterian Church after her first visit. She shook my hand at the door and said, "You've got a terrific congregation here, Mr. Murphey. So friendly. I felt like I belonged the moment I walked in."

I smiled back and said, "I know."

And I did.

Later, after everyone had gone, I stood at the door watching the last cars pull out of the parking lot—a Ford Galaxie followed by a repainted VW. I felt good. The service had finished promptly at noon. It was now, according to my Timex, 12:27. People had been milling around in front and in the parking lot, chatting, laughing, introducing themselves, enjoying one another's presence. And that wasn't an unusual Sunday. In fact, the attendance had actually been down a little.

There was a difference between our church and Phil's.

*But what was that difference?*

By the time you read this, Sara will be dead. Forty-one years old. Freckled brunette with light blue eyes. For nearly two years she had known that each day pushed her closer to her final breath. Diagnosis: cancer in four places, all inoperable. Only a matter of time, the doctor had said after she insisted on knowing.

After telling Sara the truth, the doctor left. Then followed the tears, the anger, the denial, the self pity, and then, finally, acceptance. All the commonly known stages of coming to terms with the end of life. But Sara did something else—she turned to Jesus Christ.

"Lord, I don't have a lot of days left. But I want them to be beautiful. Help me make them rich and meaningful."

The folks at Riverdale Presbyterian Church, where I serve as pastor, responded to Sara, and they responded long before they knew of her physical battle.

"You people have done so much for me," she said a few weeks ago. "I wake up every morning and thank God for being alive. I slowly look around my room and then out the window. I pause to praise God for the world he created. Then I stop and thank him for all you wonderful people at the church. You've cared so much about me. I couldn't have gone on if you hadn't been around."

Sara meant it. The folks at church had cared. Her mother had refused to see her when she heard the dreaded word *cancer*. Her alcoholic husband had left her with three months' back payments on their trailer and letters from the finance company threatening repossession of the car.

Yes, we had offered special things to Sara: we had cared.

The other day I leaned back in my chair and thought about Sara, about Phil's church, and a realization hit me. We think of caring as an emotion, a kind of feeling, an internal affair. But is it?

At times I had deep emotional feelings for Sara—sadness, pity, compassion, love, concern—and so did a lot of others. But in most of our relationship with that dying woman, we weren't conscious of a continued emotional charge.

We knew about her, so we helped. On two occasions we gave her money. One lady called her by phone every week. We offered assistance in any way she might need us. A Sunday school class took her a box of groceries from our church food pantry. Frequent telephone calls sometimes merely asked, "How are you feeling today, Sara?" One member regularly took her a cherry cheesecake. One of the shut-ins mailed her a book.

"Hey, that's right! That's caring! That's how a church really shows concern for a person."

That insight led me into other understandings. Caring *must* find expression. That expression may be as simple as speaking a few words, such as "I love you" or "I've missed you." The gift of a potted plant. A look. A warm handshake. Giving advice. Listening.

Caring can be a practical activity. When we do an act of caring, we don't always feel emotional about it. We simply do it.

That leads me to believe that caring can be planned, calculated, determined. The result can be an emotional experience.

Non-members frequently tell us about our members. They call us warm, loving, interested, concerned—all those adjectives we love to hear. And, in a lot of ways, we have that kind of congregation. We don't perfectly communicate our caring, but then who does? We've missed a lot of opportunities. We don't reach everyone.

We didn't reach Laura. She gave us the opportunity by visiting us four straight Sunday mornings. Later she told friends, "It's a cold church. I felt out of place and unwanted. Almost like you had to belong to a certain group to be important."

Part of the problem might be Laura herself. She's somewhat withdrawn. However, I'm not interested in blaming. I'm willing to admit that we failed Laura. I'm sorry about that. Several other names come to mind that we missed, too.

But we have reached others. And that encourages us to be more caring.

Jim, a professional musician who has traveled widely and is now part of our fellowship, said, "I never have been in contact with a church that showed so much love for each other. And just as loving toward strangers who come into your church."

Donna drives twenty miles each way, twice every Sunday. She said in our informal evening service, "This is like an oasis in a spiritual desert. Do you know what you've got here? I searched two years for this and now . . . now I've finally found it."

Or Ron said, "I never really had friends before—close friends—people I could open up to and tell them all about what's going on inside. This is new and really wonderful."

We're not a perfect church. As much as we want to help everyone and minister to everyone, we don't do it. In fact, we can't do it. People have a diversity of needs. Our style meets many of those needs, but certainly not all.

Some Baptists and Pentecostalists find our services too formal. Some Presbyterians and Lutherans say we're not formal enough. One man said, "I love your choir music but the rest of your music is awful." Another said, "Your music is too stiff." We can't minister to every person's need.

We know we're not perfect. But we also know that we're learning to be more sensitive to people. We want to help those who are hurting, who are lonely, who are willing for hands to reach out toward theirs. We're developing deliberate programs that respond to individual needs. We're calculating our actions to say, "We're interested in you."

In this book you'll read about our actions that result in active caring.

Part of my calling as a minister is to help provide an atmosphere where love happens. Neither I nor the members can manufacture genuine concern, but we can provide the spiritual climate where this takes place. That's what I want. My hope is that your church can take the things we're doing and modify them, adapt them, or accept them, but with the result of building a climate that shows compassion in action.

# 2.
## do you see what I see?

I hadn't wanted to go to the hospital. For several minutes, in a weakened voice I argued with Dr. Morgan on the phone. "Just call in a prescription. I'll stay in bed until I'm well. Honest."

"Okay," Zeb Morgan replied, "that's up to you. Stay home and die or get over to the hospital for that bleeding ulcer. It's your choice."

"Well, I . . . I . . ." and my voice wavered with indecision.

"I'll call the hospital and tell them you're an emergency admittance," he replied in his calm, soft drawl.

Shirley put down the phone extension, walked across the room, and picked up her sweater. "Come on, Cec. If you need any help—"

"No, I'll make it by myself," I replied stubbornly as a new wave of nausea swept over me and I vomited blood again.

Forty minutes later I lay on the white-sheeted single bed, staring at indistinguishably colored walls. I raised my head slightly to see what kind of world lay outside my window. Heavy construction equipment engaged in adding on a new wing obscured any possible view I might have enjoyed.

"Okay, Lord, I give up. I can't keep fighting and I'm not going to make a decision until you give specific directions."

Even the overcast sky on that Good Friday morning syncronized with my feelings. Weariness crept over me. Not simply because of my weakened physical condition, I decided to stop struggling. For four months I had gone through a real internal battle. I had prayed and read my Bible and prayed and prayed and prayed. No answer had come. Several opportunities had been offered, but they hadn't seemed right. The kind of church I wanted didn't seem to want me. Or if they sent a pulpit committee, I knew the situation wasn't right.

For the previous two weeks I had been planning to leave the pastorate. Why not return to teaching? I asked myself and the Lord ninety-seven times. I had taught years ago and had done a good job. I love people and have a special feeling for children. Starting pay is low, but we could survive. At least there'd be the joy of regular hours instead of the kind of existence I'd been living: on call twenty-four hours a day.

Yet I couldn't make the transition. I had received registration forms from the state department of education. I even knew of two possible openings. But just as none of the vacant churches had seemed right, neither had teaching.

I remained in DeKalb General Hospital from the morning of Good Friday until "Good Monday." Those days in isolation gave me no excuse for not getting down to business about my future.

"Lord, I'm too tired to pray about it anymore. Do whatever you want with my life."

For three years I had pastored a church in a transitional community. Blacks moved in after whites fled to the new-born suburbs. Our white island was soon surrounded by a black sea of people. Over a period of several months we discussed our plight. We tried to recruit blacks but they didn't come and many whites didn't want them. We investigated merging with another church.

"Of course," Wee Kirk Church replied, "You come over here and . . ."

"It'll work out fine. We'll both be pastors. I'll even be your assistant," another minister replied. "You sell your property and . . ."

Oddly, we had an excellent site, located on an arterial highway, but we also saw the futility of continuing to minister to a diminishing congregation. So we had voluntarily closed our doors, rather than join the white flight to the suburbs.

For the next several months I worked for our denomination, waiting for the right door to open. Several churches sent pulpit committees but none of them seemed right.

"What's wrong with me, God? Am I that hard to please?" But all the time I knew the real answer: Not God's will.

Being an activist-type who thrives under pressure, during those months I felt nearly useless. A ministry requiring about 30 hours a week was so foreign to my lifestyle. And I discovered that the more time I had on my hands the less I actually accomplished!

Then the ulcer.

During those lonely hours in the hospital, the Lord and I held a significant meeting. I surrendered to him without reservation.

"Okay, Lord, anything you want. I'm ready now. Ready to leave the pastorate or ready to stay in it for the rest of my career."

I lay in the bed all Saturday morning, interrupted only by nurses checking my temperature and blood pressure. They made certain I alternated drinking Maalox and half-and-half every hour. No calls that morning, and no visitors. No one occupied the other bed in the room. Simply the Lord and me.

Two things happened during that hospital visit. First, I acknowledged my direction: To remain in the pastorate. I fitted. I belonged. The next pastorate would be better than the last!

Second, God gave me a vision.

I didn't have an ecstatic experience or supernatural visitation. But the vision was just as real. The Lord laid out a plan for me.

In my mind I saw the kind of church I wanted to be associated with: A church of loving, caring people. Who doesn't want that kind of church? I couldn't believe anyone would consciously want a church filled with fighting and disruption.

*Love never comes automatically.* Did that thought come from my own common sense? Prompted by the Holy Spirit? I do know that the soundness of that statement shattered my tranquil thoughts.

Merely going to a new church, desiring to see love in action would never do it. I quickly thought of the New Testament churches. Paul urged them to settle internal strife.

Could ours be different? Could we prevent friction? Have less discord? Closer relationships?

*Love never comes automatically.* Everything seemed clear in that moment. We'd never have a perfect church—not even a near-perfect one. But we could have a church where people cared for each other *in spite of differences.*

A church where people retained their individuality. Where they disagreed on issues and principles, yet where no one surrendered just for the sake of unity. Where we worked together in mutual caring for each other.

My mind suddenly began clicking. I thought back over the past three years. I had done a lot of things wrong.

Like verbal lashings when meeting with the elders. They hadn't done their jobs, responsibilities to which they had pledged themselves. And I reminded them of their failures.

Or when I battled with the choir director. I won, of course, but . . .

And the church secretary? The battle lines were drawn: She had been employed by the church a dozen years before I came. I was the newcomer and in a sense, the usurper. She naturally resented some of my changes and methods. "Let's get this straight," I said on one occasion. And it took a long time to mend the broken fences with her. A lot of mistakes.

My enthusiasm began to wane.

*But you did some things right, too.*

*Oh, I suppose, I did* . . . and started to dismiss that thought.

*Why not capitalize on your successes? Why not commend the elders on what they do right? Or appreciate the effort and talents of the choir director? The church secretary puts in extra hours.*

There had been good moments at Alexander Memorial Church. People loved me. Not everyone, but I could click off names of those who genuinely cared what happened to me.

People who had come to us in our hard times. People who had given outward signs of their affection.

Like Millard and Dot. Or Ray and Dale. Val. Jim and Gay. Pug and Emily. Doran and Betty. Phil.

My mind floated backwards savoring again the flavor of tender moments. When Mrs. Anthony died, I experienced a sense of unity and common sorrow with her surviving, grown children.

Or the acceptance I felt by the "Misfits" Sunday school class I taught.

Isn't it possible to minimize the disruptive forces in a church? Couldn't we work toward unity and caring?

But how?

*By planning. By working toward goals that produce caring.*

I didn't even like the sound of those thoughts. They smacked of manipulation. A kind of spiritual seduction.

Yet it could work. If I became the pastor of a church again —as I knew by then that I would—why couldn't I work toward establishing a caring community? Toward affirming people? Toward discovering ways of alleviating guilt and avoiding verbal spankings and half-audible grumblings?

I didn't share my vision, not even with Shirley. Besides being in a half-gelled form, the whole concept seemed foolish to discuss. How do you tell of your plan to develop a particular style of church when you aren't pastor of *any* church? No blueprint unfolded. No sure-success method rested in my hands. The development of a caring congregation would unfold as I learned to know the people and as they learned to trust me. Every church is unique. What works one place fails in another. But if God directed me in this vision . . .

"Okay, God, I'll do the best I can as soon as you send me to the right church. And it will work. I know it will."

Seven weeks later I accepted a call as pastor of the Riverdale Presbyterian Church in an Atlanta suburb. I had received a mandate from the Lord: Develop a church that cares about people.

Before you read any further, I quickly confess that I stumbled a lot during the early days. I still do. But each time I learn a little and move ahead with more confidence.

The elders gave me the first problem. They had promised to set up a retreat during my first month with them. Three officers agreed to work on one project. No retreat. No project completed. At the next meeting of the board they heard strong words from me.

Driving away from the church, I felt ashamed. I had done exactly what I had promised myself not to do.

*Idiot, they know they failed. That they let you down. Did you really help them? Or did you just find an excuse for your own anger and frustration?*

I've done less of that kind of thing in the past couple of years. I don't mean vacillating every time a person disagrees with me. I let the people know my stance on issues that I feel strongly about.

I've also learned that there'll always be times and places where sincere differences arise.

Oliver Wood, a close friend and fellow clergyman, helped me greatly in that area. One day he said, "I've learned to pick my fights."

I must have given him a quizzical reply, because he went on, "A lot of times issues come up that I disagree with. But not strongly. So I shut up. What difference will they make? Will my speaking up change things? And suppose I win that one? I'll only have a harder time when the next issue arises. Why not pick the significant issues to contest?"

That seemed like a word from the Lord for me. Bend where possible and when conscience allows. But stand firm on issues where it really counts.

One issue came up about the counting of the Sunday morning offering. Most elders wanted it counted during the worship service.

"Whatever you decide is all right with me. I disagree with the practice on a theological basis. I believe we receive grace and spiritual growth by the very fact of being together in worship. Now if you still want to have the offering counted during the morning worship, I'll not fight it—but I feel that you need to know my attitude."

I lost that one. But I didn't lose the elders—a greater win!

As you read the story about a church that cares, you'll read a lot about me. Perhaps it appears that I'm doing all the forging ahead, and controlling all the activity. With most of the programs, that's exactly the way they started. But more and more activities are now going on without my involvement, such as the *FUN*damentals. They came up with a churchwide program, informed me, and tactfully asked for my input after they'd made their plans.

"I hope you don't mind..." Marcia started as she explained the caroling idea.

"Mind? I'm delighted!"

And I was.

This story doesn't end, because Riverdale Presbyterian Church still lives. We're a growing congregation, trying not to worry as much about numbers and statistics as we do about people.

People caring about people. Originally that was my vision. I kept wanting to say, "Do you see what I see? Do you grasp the possibility of a group of people committed to each other?"

My vision has now become the vision of others. And when others work toward spreading a gospel of love and care for people then I know we're succeeding!

# 3.
## it's only a name

Two elderly women sat across the table from me. I had spoken that morning at the monthly meeting of the Homemakers' Club, and then remained to eat with them.

During the conversation, they mentioned that they belonged to Glen Haven Presbyterian Church. "And we love Mr. Stover. He's wonderful," one of them said.

"You know what first impressed me about him?" the other asked. "I visited there when we first moved into the area. Then we had sickness in our home. I suppose six or seven weeks elapsed before I visited again. And when I did come back, he called me by name! Can you imagine? All the people he must meet in his work, and especially on Sunday, and he remembered me."

"Really made you feel good, didn't it?" I asked.

Both heartily agreed. "I knew right then that Ray Stover was a preacher who would care about the members of his congregation. So I joined the church."

Perhaps remembering the woman's name wasn't a great accomplishment. But it indicated something significant: Ray Stover cared enough to make the effort.

By contrast, I witnessed an experience at our own church. Ron stood at the front door of the church next to me. It was ten minutes before the service began. We welcomed visitors and chatted with people. When I saw newcomers approaching I'd nod to Ron and he would hurry over and introduce himself.

I saw Bob coming up the walk. I knew Bob had on several

occasions attended the class Ron teaches so I didn't say anything.

"Hello," he said extending his hand, "I'm Ron Davis. Glad to have you with us today. Welcome to our church."

Bob, taking it all in stride, smiled and winked at me. "Thank you."

"Glad you're with us today," Ron added. "Do you live around here?"

"Mr. Davis, I've been in your Sunday school class half a dozen times."

"Oh," Ron said, "Sorry, I'm terrible with names. I just can't seem to remember people's names."

Bob smiled back and said, "It happens to all of us."

I suspect Bob had been slightly hurt. To have been there on several occasions and not to be recognized. Not to have his name known and yet he wasn't a stranger at our church.

Remembering names and faces usually doesn't prove difficult for me. At least not when I want to remember. Of course I slip up once in awhile.

One evening my wife and I were grocery shopping. A woman kept smiling at me. I returned her smile and kept asking myself, where have I seen her before? I couldn't even give myself a hint.

At the checkout line she came up behind me. "Hello, Mr. Murphey. I'm sure you don't remember my name but I'm Agnes Miller. I met you a few months ago at a meeting of the County Emergency Clinic."

Frankly I still didn't remember her but I did say, "So good of you to remember me, Mrs. Miller."

I don't feel guilty over that incident. It only confirms that I'm not perfect and I have my troubles with names, too.

Most of the time, however, my memory works—especially when visitors come to our church. Perhaps I'm more mentally prepared to remember names then.

I'm sure that unconsciously I've devised a system. However, I'm not aware of going through any specific actions to cement a name forever in my memory. Even though I'm not conscious of how it happens, I know names and faces don't fall haphazardly into the memory bank, ready for use at the slightest effort.

I think of it like typing. I type all my manuscripts. I vaguely recall my high school days when the teacher taught us one finger and one key at a time. But if you should ask me today how my fingers move quickly across the keys, I couldn't tell you. I just do it.

Ask my wife how she learned to play the piano by ear and she'll likely give you a blank stare. No one gave her lessons. She just did it. Over the years of playing for churches and groups, she unconsciously picked up the know-how.

That's the way it is with some of us and names. No real effort. But everyone doesn't have that kind of gift. For others, it demands concentration. Hard work. A deliberate, concerted effort.

But it pays off!

It may be "only a name" but it's a lot more, too. I *am* my name.

I'm tired of introducing myself and then later have someone refer to me as Mr. Murray. That experience has occurred more than once, and I've always resented it. That kind of carelessness indicates that I'm not important enough for the other to know my name, or that the new acquaintance isn't interested in me. Neither answer is very flattering.

My name tells who I am. It's the real me. I may not like my name—and I'm not overly fond of mine—but I'm stuck with the name given me at birth. And it's been my own possession all through the years. Liking my name or not, that's the major way I affirm who I am.

Getting my name right opens the door that can lead to a good relationship with me. Get my name wrong, and we start at a disadvantage.

Ever had someone say, "I've met you before but I can't remember your name"? Chances are, he or she never really knew your name to begin with. You may have been introduced but your name slipped right past them.

But don't give up hope. There are ways you can train yourself to remember people's names.

*First,* hear the name.

I've discovered I don't always catch the name when I'm introduced. I used to be too embarrassed to ask for a repeat. Rather than troubling the other person, I think it communicates a positive interest when you say, "I'm sorry, I missed your name." It's like saying, "I sincerely do want to know your name. My hearing isn't the best so would you repeat it, please?"

Recently a distinguished looking man and his wife visited our church. I had never seen them before and I introduced myself. "I'm Roger Stuart," he said and then introduced his wife.

"So glad to meet you—uh, Stuart? Didn't Mrs. Stuart call me about two weeks ago and ask about our services and if we had nursery facilities?"

Both beamed. "Why, yes, she did call. Good of you to remember our name."

I knew I had communicated with them. They had become individuals. Not names without faces or names floating in the air, names and faces put together that gave them individuality.

*Second,* use the name.

"Mr. Rayburn, good to meet you." A simple sentence but I have already pronounced his name. I caught it. It registered. If I give it back to you, that shows that I really did hear.

A few months ago I attended a civic organization as the last-minute, fill-in speaker. The previously announced man had been taken ill. I arrived early, met the master of ceremonies, gave him my name and informed him that the program chairperson had asked me to speak.

We sat next to each other on the dias and chatted during the meal. Later, when he conducted the business session, he spent a full two minutes explaining why Dr. Hamilton could not attend. Then, just as he got ready to introduce me, he put one hand on the microphone, leaned over and whispered, "And what was your name again?"

*Third,* write the name.

I have one trick I use at the church door. We get up to a dozen visitors on any Sunday and I want to get their names straight in my mind. People push in quickly and I try to greet everyone—newcomers, members, frequent and not-so-frequent attenders. Chatting with folks as they walk inside doesn't give me time for more than a few sentences with visitors. I make sure I get their names and I repeat them to make certain I've got them right. As soon as I have a few seconds, I jot their names on the top of my church bulletin. Once I've written a name down, I know I'll remember it.

I'm a visual-oriented person. I need to *see* a name.

About once a year we have "Name Tag Sundays." For three or four weeks we give people name tags when they come into the sanctuary or their classrooms. This helps, especially when you've noticed the middle-aged couple who come every Sunday and sit in the third row, but you don't know their name. And perhaps you're even a little embarrassed to ask.

I've done something else to help me remember. When I've been caught without a pencil and have met several people in a row, I do imaginary writing with my hand.

And, it works! Once I've written it—going through the hand motion—I'm okay. I usually don't forget.

In our house, we write memory notes to each other. A note left on the kitchen table. Under a magnet on the refrigerator door. Under the clock in my bedroom. Stuck to the mirror in the bedroom.

Shirley refuses to be held responsible for a task without a reminder. It frustrates her that she has a problem with her memory. So she writes notes to herself. Then she places the note in a conspicuous place. When she sees the reminder, that triggers her into action. She insists that her brains are all on paper.

Even I write notes to myself. But once I've written the message, that's sufficient. I seldom need to look at it again. The action of putting it down on paper cements the information in my memory. It's like entering it into a computer.

I suggested this to Shirley shortly after I became pastor of a new church. She wrote down names and even jotted down a sentence or two to help jog her memory. In fact, months later, she'd say, "Paula Brent? Sure, she wore a dark blue dress with matching purse and shoes at the family night supper our first month at the church."

A name may be only a name. But it symbolizes so much more.

And I can't believe anyone can really care about Cec Murphey if he or she doesn't know that I'm not Carl Murray or Cecil McCullough or Carl Murphey!

# 4.
## a visitor comes only once

Here's one of my secret quirks: Although I've been an active church member for more than twenty years, I still feel nervous when I attend a strange church. Not merely the variations in worship. I'm self-conscious. As though I'm out of place. I worry if my tie is crooked or why-didn't-I-get-a-haircut-Thursday-as-I-had-planned? My shoes have smudges on them. I'm just plain uptight. And I haven't found many churches that allay those feelings.

That's one reason I've tried to change things in my local congregation. I'm only one person—but as pastor this gives me more opportunity. I want people to be comfortable. To relax. To sense that they can participate in our fellowship and not sit as cardboard spectators.

Over the years I've been doing some simple things to let visitors know we're interested in them as people, not merely as prospects to be courted or statistics to be counted.

*First,* twenty minutes before worship begins I go through the sanctuary and greet people already seated. I chat with them. Shake their hands. Some of them even get a hug. I always make it a point to call them by name, even if I don't know them well.

One reason I mention their names stems from a hospital incident four years ago.

Mary suffered a stroke. I visited her nearly every day. One afternoon when I tapped gently on the hospital door before going in, a voice called, "Just a minute." I heard footsteps cross the room.

Jessica opened the door. She and Mary have been friends for years. Jessica doesn't attend church as regularly as Mary, but she is a member. I knew who she was.

"I'm giving Mary a bath. Could you come back later?"

I nodded and said, "Sure, I'll drop by this afternoon. Just tell her I came by."

Several weeks afterwards, Mary commented, "Jessica says you don't even know who she is."

Surprise registered on my face.

"She told me you came to the hospital and you didn't even recognize her."

An extreme example? Perhaps, but it reminds me that a person's name is one of life's most important possessions. My using that other's name communicates that we have established some kind of relationship. It also expresses the extent of our association. To one I may say simply, "Hello, Mrs. Markham." To another it's "Hi, Janet" because we know each other better.

One of the elderly ladies of my congregation is named Ione McElroy. Shortly after I had come to this church I felt drawn to her. Perhaps because she's old enough to be my grandmother. She's warm, always smiling, and one of the friendliest people I know. I began calling her by her first name.

One morning as she left the church, she smiled and said, "You're calling me Ione, now, aren't you?"

"Is that all right?"

"Oh, yes. I love it." And she smiled at me.

*Second,* after moving quickly through the sanctuary I head for the front door. We have four ushers who serve one month at a time. I'm probably the only person in our church who knows everyone. After I have been at a church a few months, I've learned to recognize the members and spot the visitors.

As I stand in the foyer I watch for newcomers. I introduce myself as pastor and then introduce them to the closest usher or to a member of the congregation.

Usually I ask something such as "Are you new in our area or just visiting?"

"We're new in town and have just moved from Miami," a visiting family replied recently.

Another said, "I'm visiting the churches. But I've lived in this part of the country about four years."

When I introduce newcomers to an usher or to one of our members, I try to add something like, "Delta Airlines transferred the Russells here from Chicago."

This action does three things: (1) It reinforces the information they have already given me. (2) That information, transmitted to a member, provides the first step toward getting acquainted with the newcomer. (3) It puts the visitor at ease by helping him or her sense both friendliness and interest from us.

Other churches have their way to single out visitors. They receive an artificial flower or a blue ribbon on the lapel. I heard of one church where visitors were asked to sit together in a section—considered the best seats in the sanctuary. Members "sponsoring" them could sit with them, of course, but all first timers sat between rows 4 and 12 in the center section.

With most of these methods, I'm not comfortable. They set the visitors apart and only add to their discomfort—at least that's been my experience as an occasional visitor. I'd rather see the faces blended into the congregation.

During the service we have a get-acquainted time. I introduce the strangers and ask them to raise their hands. As a visitor myself, I've been more at ease in being recognized and acknowledged and then lifting my hand. Standing while everyone else is seated only calls attention to me.

My friend Brenda told me about the first Sunday she and her family visited the Stone Mountain Baptist Church. Introduction of visitors took place. The pastor said, "Will all the members stand up, please?"

Brenda and her family looked around and saw a number of other people still sitting. "It was a great feeling for us. We weren't embarrassed and after the service a lot of people introduced themselves."

At Columbia Presbyterian Church they use the Ritual of Friendship. This is a pad, placed in the rack at the end of each pew. During the early part of the service, people fill out the asked-for information: name and address and whether a visitor or member. The pad is passed along the entire pew and then back again. That gives everyone in the pew a chance to learn who the others are. Many churches use this method effectively.

A variation of the Ritual of Friendship, enacted by Bud Frimoth of the Sunset Presbyterian Church, Portland, Oregon, has a time to "Defrost the Pews."

---

**Defrosting the Pews—**
or Getting to Know You!

SUNSET PRESBYTERIAN CHURCH

By signing your name here and passing this card along the pew to others and returning it, you may open a door into friendship, call people by name, and update our church records.

| Your Name | If you are not a "regular" at SUNSET, we would appreciate this information also: | | |
|---|---|---|---|
| | Your address | Phone | Your Church |
| 1. | | | |
| 2. | | | |
| 3. | | | |
| 4. | | | |
| 5. | | | |
| 6. | | | |

To Our Visitors: "Welcome!" Whether for an hour or a lifetime, we are glad you are here and hope you will let SUNSET be your church home!

Your Responses, regarding special concerns, illness or others can be written here, or on the reverse side.

---

Some churches hold a coffee hour immediately following the morning worship. During the announcement time visitors are encouraged to remain. Ushers try to be on the lookout for newcomers and urge them to stay.

Bud Frimoth's congregation holds a coffee time. He says, "Our service of worship is so designed that folks can be going out the door before noon so their spouses won't get angry at them for 'being to church all day.' We begin our one service at

10 and close with what we call 'Part III' by 11:30. Plenty of time to get home before noon."

\* \* \* \* \* \* \*

In our service, after newcomers have been introduced with whatever bits of information I know about them, I usually say, "And now we want all of you to shake hands and greet folks near you. If you don't know your neighbors, they probably don't know you either. So give your name—you might discover a new friend today."

At the end of the service, I try to introduce all newcomers to at least one person. A lot of our members will take a minute to talk with the visitors, and will, in turn, introduce them to another family.

I've also noticed what happens when I mention that someone has only recently moved from Knoxville or San Antonio. At the end of the service, members who have lived in that area or who have good friends there, or maybe even spent their honeymoon in that city, hurry to introduce themselves.

Then we have a few folks like Skip and Suzie Cothran.

They're zealous and caring—the kind of people every church ought to have. They helped build up a Sunday school class for the under-thirty group. We began with six regulars and multiplied that figure five times.

And how did we do it? Aside from the contacts I made, Suzie and Skip invited people at work, from their apartment complex, and their friends. At church Skip and Suzie watch carefully when I introduce new people. People who look as though they might fit into that age group are met at the door.

"Hi, I'm Skip Cothran. This is my wife Suzie. . . ." And a warm friendship has a chance to come into being.

Later I see a visitor, Skip and Suzie, and one or two others from the class grouped together, chatting and getting acquainted.

"People are so friendly," Pat said at the end of her first visit.

"Hey, I was a person—not only something that fills up a seat to make the attendance look better," Phil told me.

Skip and Suzie aren't the only scouts I've got. There's Anne, a 59-year-old dynamo. She cares about people and she's always introducing herself, getting acquainted. She remembers the visitors when they come back.

We ask each newcomer to fill out a visitor's card. The following week I send a personalized letter to each one.

Here's a typical letter:

> Dear Ms. Watson,
> Thanks for worshiping with us Sunday. So glad I had a chance to meet you. And welcome to the South. Our family has been here nine years and we love this part of the country. I'm sure you will, too.
> We're glad you chose Riverdale Presbyterian Church to visit. We're not the largest church and we're far from perfect. But we care about people. Part of the Good News in Jesus Christ is that we can learn to care for each other. I hope you sensed some of that concerned interest when you worshiped with us.
> Enclosed you'll find a list of some of our activities. Feel free to participate in any that appeal to you.
> Ms. Watson, please come back and worship with us as often as you can.
> Sincerely,

Several ladies have volunteered to set up evening appointments for me. I tell them when I'm available and they call the visitors. For instance, Bernadine sets up daytime appointments for me to visit shut-ins, those recuperating from surgery, etc.

"Hello, this is Vicki Nichols from Riverdale Presbyterian Church," the conversation begins from another of my callers. She goes on to tell them she was glad they visited our church. "Mr. Murphey would like to come by and visit you one night this week if it's convenient for you."

I've discovered two extremes in follow-up work. One is the church that gets a name and hounds the person constantly with phone calls, members visiting on a weekly (or more often!) basis, and a constant pushing for commitment. That commitment may mean to the church, to Christ, or to a Sunday school class. Some respond to that type of treatment, but it's not my style of ministry.

The other extreme says, "If they like us, they'll be back." Period.

No follow-up. No carrying through. And, surprisingly enough to me, they also gain some.

I'm searching for that middle ground. To show concern—but not to push. To want people back—enough to take an active role in getting them back.

Janet came back the second Sunday morning. "Hey, it's good to see you, Janet. Hope you'll make us a habit," I said.

"I already feel part of this church. I felt like that the first time I walked inside."

She couldn't have said more wonderful words. She said what I've come to believe: I'm a visitor only once. The second time I'm part of the church family.

# 5.
## it starts with me

"O what peace we often forfeit, O what needless pain we bear . . ."

At least nine male voices (one very much off-key and one only slightly) followed Ken Campbell as he played the old favorite hymn. It was a few minutes before midnight on a Friday evening of our annual officers' training retreat. Elders from six local churches attended. We had been singing for almost an hour. After concluding the evening session we had officially dismissed for the night.

But Ken plays well and I love to sing. Apparently so did a lot of others. "Come on, let's all join in," I urged.

We had copies of a hymn book, but after the first half hour we laid the books aside, requested both newer and more gospel type songs and Ken played them. Only one or two titles threw him. And once he said, "Hey, you're really reaching back thirty years, but let's try it anyway."

When we stopped singing just before one o'clock, Evelyn commented, "It's no wonder you have an exciting church."

"You mean because I sing loud?"

"No, because you want to see people involved. You seem to enjoy getting the others participating as much as you do the actual singing."

Ralph commented, "You were standing there, leaning against the piano and as soon as someone walked by, you motioned for them to join. When we were singing out of a book, you handed them your copy of the book and picked up another one. That shows you're interested in people."

I hadn't done that consciously; but they were right, of course. And their observation fortified my own attitude. I want to draw people together. That's an underlying, ingrown principle in my lifestyle.

I want people to become part of what's going on. It disturbs me to see the loner, the wallflower, the one who sits in a row with no one else around. I respect the right of privacy but not at the expense of neglect.

I've had my turn at being outside the action circle.

I don't suppose I'll ever forget my experience in elementary school. Even then I was shorter than most of the boys in my class, very quiet, and terribly self-conscious.

Miss Kapoozie sent us from the classroom with our reading books. She instructed, "Read the story carefully. Talk about the events. Then I want you to write a play from the story." We would present the play to the entire class.

Martha, a platinum blonde with brown eyes and tiny freckles, led the group. "Bobby, you can be the father. You're tall and handsome. And Mary Anne, since you're tiny, you can be baby Jane."

One by one she gave out the parts. Dark-haired Dave with long lashes and shining bright eyes received the part of the boy next door—the part with the most lines to read.

"What about me?" I finally asked after all the parts had been given out.

"Oh, well, you can be the dog. All you have to do is follow as we walk around."

I didn't cry. After all, boys don't cry. But I had been left out of the reading group. And it hurt.

I noticed others in our class who were always the left-outs. Jimmy Larson because he was fat. Laura Bishop whose clothes were always dirty, and often too short. Manuel Alcado, the only Mexican in our class.

"Miss Kapoozie," I approached the teacher one day at noon, "I want to do a play. I mean a real kind of play. When I'm in my reading group I never get a part and neither does Manuel or Jimmy or Laura. Couldn't I find a story in a different book and let us be our own group?"

"But you're all part of reading groups—I grouped you—" and then she stopped, "Hmm, that might be a good idea. Why don't you see what you can find when we visit the school library Wednesday? You can do it for us later this week."

"I've already found one. In our library book, I mean. I found it last Wednesday. And—there are parts for all of us and—"

The next day I made my company work quietly in the corner of the classroom during the entire lunch period. They learned to read their lines as well as grade schoolers could. Immediately after lunch, Miss Kapoozie let us do our play.

Afterwards she said, "You did very well. I'm going to talk to the other teachers and see if you can't do your play for other classes, too."

And we did.

That didn't solve my problems about being outside the group, but it did something for me. From then on I became aware of distinctions of the in group and the outcasts. Although not conscious of making a decision, in reflection I realize that I've frequently looked for ways to include outsiders in activities.

That single incident in grade school—has that been the major reason I've been concerned about developing a style of including others? I think so.

I never became the top leader in any of my classes; I really didn't want that. But I realize now that throughout my school years, during my military service, and my adult activities, I've tried to draw in the loner, the neglected, the ignored.

That ties in with another realization: People in my congregation can't be expected to care unless I set the example.

Shortly after Shirley and I married we attended a midwestern church. We heard the most scorching sermons—not about punishment for the wicked, or a fiery hell. But poor Brother Howard! I don't think he ever found anything right with the world, with people, or with the church.

He was the kind of man who pounded the pulpit, frowned,

and cried out, "God calls us to love people!"

One of the last sermons we heard him preach before we moved our membership concerned winning people to Christ. He pointed out that we, the members, were sheep and he the shepherd. He quoted verse after verse informing us that we were "sheep of His pasture." His next point underscored that, naturally, sheep give birth to sheep. Shepherds don't. "That's their task—the sheep reproduce and other sheep come into existence. The shepherd guides and feeds the sheep."

From that doubtful premise (after all, as a Christian, wasn't he a sheep, too?) he produced a dozen Scriptures commanding us to go out and witness for Jesus Christ. He never told us of *his* obligations.

And, frankly, no warmth ever made itself felt in that church. I frequently heard bickering. Sometimes words heated up the place. Once they almost had a split over the location of the kitchen in their soon-to-be-completed building.

When Brother Howard left, a congregation of disgruntled, frowning people stayed behind. And yet I heard people say, "At one time this used to be a friendly church. The kind of place where everyone really liked everyone else."

I still think of that church once in awhile. The pastor was only one person but he influenced the rest. He set the example.

And what was his example? It really became a message of "Let George do it. It's not my responsibility. Someone else ought to bring people to Jesus Christ."

It begins with the leaders. As a pastor, it begins with me. It can even begin with you—one of the seemingly insignificant ones.

W. A. and Edna came to Riverdale Presbyterian Church years ago. I don't know a great deal about how things were when they came. But it was a small town, a family-oriented, family-dominated church where two or three families made the important decisions.

W. A. and Edna changed a lot of that attitude and ingrownness. They changed people by being open and outgoing. As newer people came into the church, they went out of their way to welcome them, to make them feel part of the church family.

They knew where loving care had to start: with number one. It begins with me. Writing *it begins with me* doesn't mean merely beginning with the pastor!

W. A. and Edna moved to Florida two years ago. They began attending a church near their new home.

"At first, we thought the people were just cold toward strangers," W. A. said. "Then we began to realize that they just weren't particularly friendly to each other. Yet when you talked to anyone individually, each was kind and interested."

After their fourth Sunday, W. A. and Edna began going to Sunday school class and made it a point to go around the room and shake hands with every person and chat for a few minutes.

"You ought to see that class now," Edna beamed. "Why, they're all so friendly. Now they're already talking to each other before we even get there."

"Most people want to be friendly," W. A. said. "They sometimes just need a push in the right direction."

\* \* \* \* \* \* \*

You want a warm, caring church?

It begins with you. With me.

But I wouldn't feel right to stop there, because the new question is *how*. How do I become loving, caring, concerned? How do I become the disciple of Jesus Christ so that people know I'm his?

Part of that answer means setting the right example. I can't expect people to be reaching out to others unless they realize I'm reaching out.

During my high school days I worked for a short time at a soda fountain. My boss, one day, was cleaning up, doing a lot of menial tasks that we who worked for her were expected to do.

"Hey, Ruth, you shouldn't do that. You're the boss. I'll do it."

She smiled but continued working. "I have a rule. I never ask an employee to do what I won't do myself."

No wonder we all loved Ruth. She was not only the right kind of boss, but the right kind of leader.

At our church several people's names pop into my mind. People who genuinely care about other people. When members are sick and in the hospital, five or six people often get there before I do!

That's one step in getting a congregation of caring people: set the example for others to follow.

A second part of the answer says we have to receive something ourselves before we can pass it on.

The other night I paid a pastoral call on LuAnne. She's single, twenty-eight, and plain. And very lonely. She's made two prolonged trips to a mental hospital because of acute depression.

LuAnne's coming out of all that now. And here's what worked for her.

First, she had to receive something herself before she could respond. She began attending a Sunday school class in our church. We call it the Bridge Builders (they want to build bridges between groups and people in the church). LuAnne felt accepted. The class is open and sharing. She cautiously told one or two things about herself. People responded.

At the end of the class Polly walked over to her and said, "I'm glad you came today. And I'm really happy to meet you. Come on and sit in church with us."

Other things—the singles group responded to LuAnne. And even Denny, a young single, saw her, met her, and even dated her occasionally.

So, first LuAnne began responding to love and care.

But that wasn't enough. She had to learn. And she learned by accepting herself.

"God doesn't create junk. If I'm a creation of God, I'm worthwhile," she says to herself. Or she looks in the mirror and says, "I'm gifted. God has given me talents. I'm not a nobody. I am somebody."

Sentences and phrases like this keep flowing through her thoughts each day. Call it self-hypnosis. Call it anything you like. But I call it self-affirmation.

Then she began to think about her ability. On an earlier visit she had said, "I don't like me. I've even thought of killing myself. Wouldn't the world be better off without nobodies like me?"

You know what she said the other night? "Mr. Murphey, see this dress I'm wearing? I made it myself. I cut out the pattern, sewed every stitch. The girls at work all raved about it." And it looked fine.

"For a nobody, LuAnne, you've done quite well."

Then she laughed—one of the first laughs I had heard in my months of knowing her. "I'm not a nobody. I'm even beginning to like myself. Not all the time, but most of the time. And that's a step forward, isn't it?"

And that night she called Jane, a member of the singles' group. "Just thinking of you. I was a little lonely and wondered if you were lonely, too."

Self-acceptance—a necessary first step.

And behind that lies the underlying belief that God loves me. His loving me means an unreserved acceptance of me as worthwhile, as significant, as loveable.

Then, and only then, can we respond to people. Only then can we allow people to love us. And people are always reaching toward every one of us. We need to learn to say, "Thank you" instead of, "Oh, you can't mean *me.*"

We accept ourselves, with our gifts and liabilities, our perfections and our smudges. We enjoy being who we are. And we're happy in being ourselves.

When that all comes together in our heads and hearts, then we reach out, too. We reach for others and they respond. And their response makes us stronger in our self-affirmation.

\* \* \* \* \* \* \*

I had visited nearly an hour with Pete. Although a member he had not been active for years. But he still kept up with our activities through our newsletters and friends who attended faithfully.

"Things are going great these days, I hear," he said. "I'm glad."

"Pete, I'm happy at Riverdale. The people have been so loving. And it's easy to respond to them."

He chuckled and I remember his blue eyes looking straight into mine. "It's because you're easy to respond to."

Pete said one of the most encouraging words I'd heard all that week. He made me feel affirmed. Appreciated. Cared about. But even more, that statement strengthened me. It encouraged me to move ahead in opening myself up to people. To keep reaching out and letting people know that I honestly cared. To keep saying, "You're important."

I've arrived at no destination or resting place where I say, "I've got it all worked out now." I'm still moving forward. And I'm even more excited about life and about the influence of Jesus Christ in my life than ever before. I may not have arrived at my destination, but I'm traveling down the right road.

A pop tune of my boyhood days flashed into my mind as I sat typing this chapter. I don't recall all the words, but the song ends something like:

> the greatest thing is to love
> and be loved in return.

And the more I love, the more I find people loving me.

But it starts with me.

# 6.
# lots of love to share

Like solving brain teasers? Here's one.

Two hundred people will sit inside an oblong-shaped room for sixty minutes every Sunday morning. During that hour they need to be affirmed and loved. At the same time, they need guidelines for living until they return a week later.

That's the situation. How do you find a way to help 200 people (including yourself) during that one hour?

In the Presbyterian Church we have a usual order of worship. We vary it, but it's not greatly different at Riverdale Presbyterian than it is at the First Presbyterian Church of Atlanta. And it's not greatly different from Grace United Methodist, First Baptist, or the Faith Assemblies of God. We have music, preaching, reading the Scriptures, and the offering. Some churches have services lasting two hours. A few can get you in, hand out the gospel, and you're standing in the parking lot within 49 minutes.

At Riverdale Presbyterian Church we don't communicate caring perfectly. But we're working on it. I'm going to tell you what happens on a typical Sunday morning in our church. I'll share also the rationale for these activities.

Marcia and Ben joined our church recently. She said to me, "You did something that first Sunday that impressed me so much that I've never gotten over it."

Of course I wanted to hear *what* so I relaxed in my chair and waited for her to continue.

"I grew up in church. I never went through a period when I

didn't want to attend. But never—never—did I have a minister at the door to greet me when I first came to church. Like that first Sunday, you stood there and introduced yourself. You may have said you were the pastor—I didn't hear it—and you acted so friendly and introduced us to some others. Ten minutes later you walked in with the choir—well, it nearly blew my mind!"

"I thought it was wonderful, and I told Ben. So many preachers greet us at the end of the service, but you were the first one to greet me when I came in. I felt you were interested."

These words tell what I'm trying to do in our worship services. I want to create an atmosphere. An attitude. A spirit. If love and friendliness bloom in a congregation, people sense something's alive and growing.

I've had one complaint over this change in style. One member said, "I used to go to church ten minutes early so I could sit quietly in the sanctuary and meditate. Now there's such a hum of noise—people chatting and greeting each other—that it's impossible for me to sit quietly and not join in."

Someday we'll have the answer to that one. But I'd rather have the cacophony of caring voices than the cold silence of indifference.

Our services begin like traditional Presbyterian services. We incorporate items in our worship such as the Lord's Prayer and the Apostles' Creed. That's done on purpose. However, I like change. I enjoy new things happening, and exploring innovative ideas. But I also realize people's need for security.

My feeling is that some people (and I suspect this applies especially to the over-40 crowd like myself!) need a sense of solidarity. I can explore, experiment, change in certain areas so long as I keep the foundations sure. And for many, the foundations revolve around the creeds, the hymns, and the sermon. That presents no problem for me.

And for people coming into our services for the first time, I want a sense of familiarity there. Too many changes would make it difficult for a newcomer to feel at ease. But within the given structures we try to express an atmosphere of caring about people.

Our theology and practice in a typical morning worship program can be briefly explained as follows.

PRAYER. Since the concept of prayer involves so much in the life of any growing and caring church, I'm devoting a whole chapter in this book to the subject.

But I have adopted several guidelines for prayer in our congregation.

First, the preacher doesn't do all the praying. Prayer is the offering of ourselves and of our needs to God.

During a period when I was not a pastor, I sat through services at several churches. One Sunday I discovered that I had completely outlined an article during the protracted prayer by the man of the cloth. At one church where we attended during my years as a public school teacher, Shirley confessed, "I find myself planning my next week's schedule during that fifteen minute interlude. I unconciously turn him off and really don't hear his rambling monologues anymore."

Second, praying is a heart-exercise and not merely a head activity. I want to teach people to let it come from inside and not merely spew prepared or memorized words that glide across the tongue with little meaning.

Third, I'm trying to find ways to increase our sense of community in praying. So much praying in worship dictates that we bow our heads, close our eyes, and listen while someone else prays. I find little sense of fellowship there.

Fourth, people need instructions on how to pray. Our traditional praying in formal worship settings denies the sense of spontaneity. Why not pray in the way we want to teach people to pray? That is, why not set the example by doing it in a relaxed, informal way?

Those are the principles I've tried to work with. The next chapter incorporates them in our attempts at a bona fide community prayer life.

THE ANNOUNCEMENTS. Although I've heard people (including preachers) speak of this part of the service as either boring or an interruption, I don't. It can be a creative time. It helps highlight the hour for me and changes the pace of the rest of the service. Until this point, the service has been rather formal. Now people relax. Occasionally a member stands up in the sanctuary to plug a coming event or get volunteers for a new program.

A few months ago we had a member from each of the five adult Sunday school classes stand up and share for two or three minutes what was happening in that particular class. They wanted other adults to know that Sunday school can be exciting, fun and meaningful, and not merely an activity for children.

When the congregation has responded to needs, I commend them during the announcement time. For example, they recently responded to a plea for food and clothing for a young widow with three children. Several boxes of food were taken to the home, clothes for each of the children, and a check for fifty dollars.

Several times since I've been at Riverdale I've said simply, "Thanks for your support. Sometimes being a pastor can be a thankless and lonely position. You have helped me by your encouragement and support. I appreciate *you* and your ministry to me."

By standing out in front I've already personally greeted almost everyone in the sanctuary—except, of course, those who arrived after 10:55. At that time I leave, go to the rear of the sanctuary, and have prayer with the choir.

During the announcement time I introduce visitors by name, asking them to raise their hands, making sure people in the congregation see them. If I spot other visitors, I say, "And I believe this young couple sitting next to the Crofts is new. Would you tell us your name?"

Then I say, "We like people to know that we're friendly. We care about people here. We believe in smiling, shaking hands, and even speaking to each other. So now I'd like you to greet the people sitting near you. Next to you. In front of you. Behind you. And if you don't know their names, probably they don't know yours either. Just think: you might start a lifelong friendship this morning."

I turn and chat a few seconds with the choir. For two full minutes cheerful voices reverberate through our sanctuary. A few people even get out of their pew and cross the aisle!

THE CHILDREN'S SERMON. I have a special time where I give a visualized, five-minute message for children. (This is dealt with in a later chapter.) While I call it a *children's* sermon, I know it reaches beyond the ten-year-olds.

The other night Ed and I visited Billy and Linda. It was our first visit to their home. They had attended our services twice.

"You know what I like best about the whole service?" Billy smiled self-consciously. "The children's sermon."

"You must really love those children," Linda said.

"I also love their parents," I replied.

Linda smiled again. "That shows, too."

THE SERMON. This can be the dullest time in the spiritual week. I work at avoiding the sin of boredom.

*First,* I preach short sermons. Twenty minutes is long enough. Take a tip from television. Ever count the minutes between commercial breaks? Roughly ten minutes on prime time during the movies and specials, even shorter during newscasts and sports events.

*Second,* I illustrate. Here's the way I began a sermon recently, called "Taking a Guilt Trip."

> One morning the phone rang at 8:05. I was alone at church and I answered. I felt the pressure of a heavy work load ahead of me and almost wished I didn't have to answer.
>
> It was an old friend. She chatted several minutes about what was going on in her life. Finally she explained why she was calling. And then—we had been on the phone twenty minutes—she said, "What's going on with you? You're always doing something exciting and I'd like to hear."
>
> Frankly, I didn't feel like telling her about the exciting things. I felt only the frustration of being in the office early, concerned about getting a lot of work done and losing twenty minutes of that valuable time.
>
> "Can I call you back later? Right now I'm swamped and—"

Before I finished my statement, I heard the coolness in her voice as she said, "Yes, I understand."
Click! Down went her receiver.
Now I hadn't acted wrongly—so far as I know. I had been honest with my friend. But I had to fight a terrible sense of guilt. She was hurt; her voice gave that away. I hadn't intended to hurt her . . . and I felt guilty.

From there I began talking about the characteristics of guilt.

Illustrating isn't just telling stories. I try to make all my points concrete and easily understood.

For instance, in the same sermon I wanted to point out how people produce guilt in us. We often produce guilt by blaming. "I sat here all afternoon and you didn't call. . . ." Or by gentle cohesion, "Why, all the Christians in the community are giving to the special offering for War on Poverty."

Caring means not only serving meals which are delicious but well cooked and in attractive containers. If I care about you, I won't force feed or say, as mothers of a past generation did of home remedy medicines, "I know it tastes awful, but it's good for you."

*Third,* my sermon is affirming. So much of the preaching I listened to during my early years in the pew all had a sound of negativism. I kept hearing what was wrong with me. Our failures visualized and verbalized. Sinner. Reprobate. Words like that poured from the pulpit.

Perhaps a lot of my preaching is merely reaction to that style. But I believe it's far more.

During my first year of teaching, Jeffrey came into my class. *Incorrigible* was the word most teachers had previously applied to him.

"Make him stand in the hallway," one teacher recommended.

"Just place his desk in a corner of the room," another suggested.

Then I met Jeffrey. Much smaller than other sixth-graders, he looked as though he belonged in third grade. He never looked at my face when talking to me. Jeffrey kept his voice low, making me strain to hear it.

I prayed about handling Jeffrey. The other teachers hadn't exaggerated about his conduct. And he *did* behave when I yelled at him or punished him.

*But what if I took time to love him?* I tried a new tactic. Whenever Jeffrey did anything right, even the slightest show of interest, of participation, I found ways of letting him know I noticed. A smile. A wink. A pat on his shoulder.

By the end of the year, Jeffrey amazed all of us by his almost genius with math. He reasoned abstractly and seemed to do it effortlessly. After conferring with a seventh grade math teacher, we allowed him to work on advanced problems. Finally he went through the entire seventh grade math book during the last three weeks of school. I still had a few problems with Jeffrey, but no more than with any other child.

And what made the change? We took positive action rather than defensive reaction to his behavior.

That's the kind of tactics I try with a congregation. Not as a gimmick, because people instinctively know if caring doesn't come from the heart.

Perhaps people need spanking, bawling out, denouncement. I'm just not comfortable doing that.

In the Old Testament the prophets often spoke in those negative tones. Jeremiah rebuked. Hosea laid it on thick. Ezekiel didn't do badly either. But it seems to me that the primary office of the prophet was to call the people back—back to God, back to the faith, back to righteousness.

As a modern-day pastor, I have also the responsibility to nurture, to heal, *and* to rebuke. If I err in going too far in the wrong direction, I'd rather it be in my lack of rebuke. I'd rather proclaim the positive, affirmative gospel. I'd rather they hear of God's love and forgiveness. Grace means more to me than judgment.

And I suspect that most people know only too well their own sinfulness and guilt. They don't need more experiences of being labeled wretched and evil. I do think they need a lot more said about their acceptability to God.

My sermons deal with topics like "Loving Myself" or "Handling Jealousy" or "Struggles to Live Like a Christian."

*Fourth,* they're as honest as I know how to be. I don't tell my success stories—at least I keep them at a minimum. I do tell a lot of my *unsuccess* stories.

Here's a transcription of part of a recent sermon:

> Last week I got angry over a trivial matter. A salesman felt the brunt of it. And it was my fault—my impatience and my rudeness. Five minutes after leaving the store I went back and apologized. I felt so miserable about my behavior. I had fouled up. Now God didn't make me lose my temper or force me to apologize. I did it all by myself. But God did give me enough grace to go back and apologize!
>
> Despite my failures—despite the fact that I've never quite arrived at any place of spiritual perfection—I'm trying to walk in the right path.

Brady had been a member of my church for almost a year before he stopped by the house one evening. "I appreciate your sermons. You're human. You make mistakes like the rest of us. I always got the impression before that preachers didn't have the kind of spiritual problems the rest of us have. Or else that you always had victory over all of them."

I'm glad my humanness showed. It helps me identify with people. And identity leads to acceptance and fellowship.

* * * * * * *

In many ways our Sunday morning worship services fit into traditional modes. It's not the outline from the church bulletin that tells our story but the attitudes, the working out of activities around and through the formal structures of worship. We're constantly trying new avenues to project our caring.

We're discovering that the more we care, the more love we have to share!

# 7.
## when *we* pray

"This may sound dumb to you," he said as he looked down at his hands, "I'm an officer and I've been a Christian a long time, but...." His voice paused and he finally said, "I've finally learned to pray. Sounds dumb, I know, but...."

"If you've learned something, Roger, that can't be dumb," I answered.

"It's what we do on Sunday mornings. I listen and get a lot of help out of the way we pray together. But, know what?" He grinned self-consciously. "I guess prayer always seemed so hard, like having to have some kind of special ability, but you've made it easy. It's really just talking to God, isn't it?"

Roger's remarks encouraged me. I had been trying to evaluate the effectiveness of our style of prayer. He gave me an honest, unsolicited answer.

Frequently when I visit with newcomers in their home, they refer to the prayer time we share. I'm convinced that we're on the right track.

The bulletin reads simply "The Congregation at Prayer." I don't call it the pastoral prayer. I did until a couple of summers ago when we vacationed in the Northeast.

The pastor announced the pastoral prayer. He began with a lengthy introduction of our unworthiness to approach a holy God but that Christ had made a new and living way. After five minutes of listening to his words of praise and thanksgiving, I thought, surely he's almost finished. After seven minutes, according to my watch which seemed to move extremely slow that morning, I convinced myself that he really had to be near the end. After all, we had already covered the needs of the local congregation and the world-wide churches of Jesus Christ. Wrong again. He totaled 18 minutes.

And the man in front of us didn't lift his head after the prayer. Did I hear muffled snores later on? At least he remained in the right position to emit those noises.

As I sat there, hoping to get through with the prayer, a thought struck me. *That's the trouble. He's only doing what the bulletin says.* The pastoral prayer means the pastor praying. The people sit passively and listen. Perhaps some of the more spiritual ones are mentally adding *amen* to everything.

It was almost like eavesdropping while a man had his private devotions. We were audience, not participants. Of course, that might say something about the level of my spirituality. It might also say we need to rethink our public prayers.

In our church bulletins we write "The Congregation at Prayer." It becomes more than mere word change. As we begin this part of the service, I usually mention two or three special concerns. "Young Vicki Mobley is back in the hospital. She's only 14 and this time they have discovered a non-malignant growth on the tip of her spine. Our nominating committee for church officers requests us to pray for them as they complete their task."

Then we actually begin our congregational prayer. This is how a typical Sunday morning prayer begins.

"As we pray, I'd like you to talk to God yourself, using your own words. I'm going to suggest matters for prayer and then pause for you to talk silently to God.

"God cares for this world he created. Thank God for our world . . . the everyday beauty of trees and stars . . . of springtime and summer showers. . . ."

The rationale: 1 Peter 2:9–10 tells us that we are all priests, all able to offer prayer to God. In this way, I am attempting to say "You can pray yourself. You can make contact with God. You don't need a minister to do all the praying."

It's also my way of helping people pray. "I don't know how

to pray." That statement comes often to ministers. I hope this shows them how.

After this I suggest that we thank God for people. "People play significant roles in our lives. Our friends . . . parents . . . teachers . . . co-workers . . . people who've made our lives healthier and happier. Let's mention them by name and thank God for their presence in our lives."

We have a section of time devoted to forgiveness. "Let's ask the Holy Spirit to speak to each one of us, to make us aware of our sins. Our shortcomings . . . then confess and ask forgiveness . . . for the harsh words we've said this week . . . for feelings of jealousy and hostility. . . ."

Most public prayers stay on a general level. They say things like, "Forgive us for our sins" and "Make us more like Jesus Christ." I like prayer to have a more personal touch.

This came to me in an almost laughable situation during my missionary service in Africa. Five African pastors, my wife, and I conducted an open air meeting at Migori market. We sang nearly an hour, pausing occasionally for each one to give short exhortations to come to Jesus Christ.

As we prepared to close, one of the pastors gave an invitation for people to turn to Jesus Christ. Thirty people came forward and knelt down. The pastor prayed and then said, in the Luo language, "I want you to repeat after me," and he prayed a few phrases at a time. All thirty voices echoed his words.

He thanked God for salvation in Jesus Christ and for the opportunities we have to know him. Then he moved into the confession of sin. "Thank you, God, for forgiving my sin of adultery . . . for delivering me from the curse of liquor. . . ."

As I opened my eyes and looked at the crowd, at least ten of them were children. I suspected they had no idea what the word *adultery* meant. They only repeated words the pastor gave them.

If prayer really means that we're in contact with God himself, then why don't we pray about our *individual* sins? And who else knows them but God and ourselves? I give them suggestions for personalized prayer.

I conclude the confessional time by a statement such as: "If you confessed to God, here's wonderful news. You're already forgiven in Jesus Christ! You're free from those sins."

Other areas of prayer suggest praying for greater harmony and love among our congregation, greater concern for people outside our church who need our love.

"Pray for me as your pastor. Ask God to lead me by His Spirit as I attempt to lead this church."

I think it's important to insert that request. I need the affirmation and sense of support every bit as much as the people in the pew. But even more important, they need to know their prayers are important and that we labor together.

Asking them to pray for me reminds me of an incident in the life of Moses (cf. Exodus 17:8–13). The Amalekites attacked the Jews and Joshua led the Jewish army. Moses stood on the mountaintop and "whenever Moses held up his hand, Israel prevailed; and whenever he lowered his hand, Amalek prevailed." (v. 11)

Then Moses tired. "So they took a stone and put it under him, and he sat upon it, and Aaron and Hur held up his hands, one on one side, and the other on the other side; so his hands were steady until the going down of the sun." (v. 12)

It's a way of saying, "I'm your leader, but I can't lead without your help. I need you."

In a former church, on a Sunday morning with over 200 present, I asked a question in the middle of my sermon. "How many of you pray regularly for me as your pastor?" Not a single hand went up. I would imagine that's about average for most churches. And if leaders believe it's important for the prayers of the congregation to be with them, that's another area we need to teach people about.

Near the end of the prayer time, I say, "Now pray for yourself. You're a unique person. Each of you. God made you. He loves you. You're worthwhile. I'd like you to say something like, "God, thank you for me. . . . Thank you that I'm worthwhile. . . ."

Lynn talked to me after her fourth visit to our church. "That really helps me, Mr. Murphey, when you ask us to pray for ourselves. I've always felt like I didn't have anything good about me. I've even wondered sometimes why God let me be born. I don't want to die, but I've always felt I was no good. No talents. Nothing to give anyone. But praying that way on Sunday mornings helps me so much."

"Lynn, I really believe we all need that lesson."

"I'm learning. Now I'm looking at myself. There are things I can do. And I feel better about myself all the time."

I remember when George came up to me. "I almost didn't come to church today. I felt rotten. Just plain useless. But when you asked us to thank God for ourselves—it lifted me up. It really helped just to look at me as a worthwhile individual."

That concretely states what I believe the congregation at prayer ought to do. It ought to affirm. To encourage. To strengthen.

I know that everyone doesn't respond to my emphasis upon the self-affirmation. That's why I keep doing it every week. If people have a negative image of themselves, it may have come about because they kept hearing explicitly or implicitly, that they were useless. I think they need to hear the other side repeated endlessly.

And a few times it's been hard to follow through on that. To always emphasize the positive and to show caring.

I'm the pastor. Sometimes I see people in the congregation who haven't been there in three months, or who I know aren't being faithful. Or, hardest of all, an elder who's irregular in duties, attendance, and giving. What an opportunity to get at people like that!

One day Roy and Betty came, after nearly two months' absence. Roy had volunteered for several projects with the Men of the Church and dropped them, forcing someone else to carry his load. Even though an officer in his Sunday school class, he had simply stopped attending.

Roy and Betty had slipped in late. What a temptation to blast away at unfaithfulness or lack of commitment.

Later, at the door he said, "I almost didn't come back to church. I've let everybody down. God mostly. But also this church. The people. I came back today and expected you to chew me out. And in the prayer time when you asked us to pray for ourselves—that really got to me. I've settled it now. Betty and I are going to get back into things and follow up on our promises."

I stood there, giving silent thanks to the Lord. I had battled internally at first. *Thanks, Lord, for winning over my feelings. You settled it with Roy. Your Spirit brought conviction.*

Obviously, at times pastors need to confront people, to make them face facts. I prefer to do that when I'm alone with them. For me, the pulpit isn't the place to spew out anger and bombard people with my frustrations. For this period of time together I want to emphasize concern for people and for each other.

On Sunday nights prayer takes on an entirely different form. At a recent evening service, one of the men cried as he said, "I need your help and your prayers. The preacher's been asking us to thank God for ourselves and to love ourselves. I don't love myself. I know that I need to learn. If I can't love myself, I can't really love anyone else, can I?"

Responses like his convince me that we're heading in the right direction. I ask people to talk to God themselves. The Holy Spirit can speak back to them. Then prayer becomes a dialogue. When that happens, people know that God cares about them!

# 8.
## where-are-you? time

In the middle of our evening service, Richard stood up to make a prayer request.

You have to understand that Richard is a heavy-set, gruff-voiced truck driver. Words don't flow easily with him and he often talks in choppy sentences, especially when he's nervous or excited.

That night his voice sounded both gruff and choppy. "Cec, I have a prayer request."

"Sure."

"And I want Bob to pray."

I shrugged my shoulders, "Okay, Richard. What is it?"

"I want Bob to pray for you and Shirley. We love you. You're always doing so much for everyone. We just take you for granted. So I want us to pray for you."

Richard's request told me several things. First, we have provided the kind of trusting relationship in the evening service where people speak freely. Richard isn't the type who normally speaks up.

Second, the request showed a sensitivity to others. I hadn't shared my need—which at that time was definite but not acute. His speaking up happened at an appropriate time.

Third, the preacher isn't merely a professional, always on top of his problems. They recognized me as one of them even though I was the leader.

Richard sat down and Bob prayed. Moistness collected in my eyes. Two years ago I would have been uncomfortable, and would have fought showing any emotional response and allowing my feelings to show through. But it was okay with this group. I had learned to trust, too.

What a wonderful feeling—me, the pastor. *They* prayed for *me*. An expression of genuine love.

That's only part of the reason I tell people that on Sunday nights at our church the Lord ministers *to* me. I have my role, I'm visible in the service, but it's *our* service together. I leave feeling built up, encouraged. And most of all, I know the people who attend on Sunday nights love me.

Here's a rundown on what happens during our evening service.

First, the attendance runs from 25 to 60 people. Several of those people have active memberships in other churches, such as Wayne, an active Methodist, and Mary, who never misses Sunday morning in her Baptist church. But for them and a few others, Sunday night at our church focuses in on the kind of service they need.

We make no great effort to publicize this service. The attendance has been growing mostly through word of mouth. Martin said, "If I had to miss a lot and could only attend one service, this is the one I'd attend."

Sunday evenings have a special focus to minister to people who want an atmosphere of warmth and active caring.

We don't meet in our sanctuary, but in our fellowship hall. We set up semi-circles of chairs around the piano with a space for a small lectern.

Second, the smallness gives the sense of closeness. We feel that genuine warmth is generated during this hour together.

We have a traditional beginning, usually with prayer and then our music. Very contemporary music is mixed with a few old-timer hymns.

Bob leads two or three songs from an older hymnbook, often asking for requests. The choices? Often "In the Garden" or "Amazing Grace." And it's not the older crowd asking for these, either!

I usually lead singing after that. We vary our songs. We

might start with a chorus such as "The Joy of the Lord Is My Strength," a simple, 4/4 tune to which we clap our hands. And a rediscovered song that gets asked for almost every week is "Victory in Jesus." We've learned a lot of the Bill Gaither pieces and keep looking out for new music to express our worship and fellowship in Jesus Christ.

We have an overhead projector. Every few weeks we find a new song we like so we write the words on the acetate.

We even do an action song occasionally, such as "If You're Saved and You Know It, Shout Amen."

The first few times after we began clapping I said, "Jesus Christ sets us free to worship. Clap your hands if you want. If you'd like to clap but feel too inhibited, then tap your feet."

I don't look around but I suspect that almost everyone claps.

"It's meaningful to me," Joe Ann said. "I'm learning that worship doesn't have to be stiff and dull. What's wrong with clapping your hands? The Old Testament speaks about it in place after place."

And Ron added, "That's been the best part for me. I used to worry about how I looked or what people thought of the way I dressed. Now I come in here without a coat or tie, clap my hands and no one seems to notice."

A few months ago I taught "Fill My Cup, Lord." I especially focused on this hymn because I believe our senses ought to be involved in our worship to Jesus Christ.

Since the words of this actually are a prayer, we sing the chorus prayerfully. But we do something else.

"Think of yourself as a cup—a small demitasse or a large loving cup or any size you want. When we get to the chorus, lift your cup to the Lord."

> Fill my cup, Lord. I lift it up, Lord.
> Come and quench this thirsting of my soul.

I glanced quickly and noticed that almost everyone had lifted hands as I had suggested.

This is part of the freeing in our service. We attempt to create a relaxed atmosphere. I frequently take off my coat.

Everyone dresses casually. Sometimes Donna or Betty will lead the singing. People speak up with requests. When I'm out of town, we don't bring in a guest speaker; one of them teaches or preaches.

But the best part of the service comes after the hymns. I call it "Where are you?"

"Okay, folks, where are you? What's happening in your lives? Anything going on that you want to share with us? A blessing? Answered prayer? A good experience? Or do you have a prayer request? A need?"

That's when the action takes place.

Thelma's a fiftyish wisp of a woman whose eyes light up. She speaks staccato style. "Oh, I just have to praise the Lord tonight. Gene's blood pressure got dangerously high recently. I called Frances and Donna for prayer. You know what? He's fine now."

A few murmur "Praise the Lord," not too loudly and some quite timidly. Someone told me that the deaf sign for "Praise the Lord" is to hold your hand like the "one-way" sign—fingers closed with right index finger extended and then the hand making a circular motion. Several people do that. "This is for those of you who want to express praise to the Lord but are reluctant to make a joyful noise."

"I need a job," Wanda said.

Five or six people sitting near her reached over and laid their hands on Wanda while Martin prayed audibly.

We frequently lay hands on people who make prayer requests and we do it for definite reasons.

First, we believe it's Scriptural. Throughout the New Testament we find frequent references to laying hands on people when praying for them (Matt. 8:3, 14:31; Mark 1:41; Acts 6:6, 8:17–18, 9:12, 11:30, 19:11, 28:8, etc.).

Second, we believe that human hands communicate. In the Old Testament one of the concepts of laying on of hands was that of transferrence. For instance, on the Day of Atonement the high priest confessed the sins of the entire nation. *He laid his hands on the scapegoat.* Symbolically, the goat now had received the sins of the people.

For me the laying on of hands symbolizes the transferrence of faith, love, and a sense of being at one with the needy person.

Occasionally, the request will be an enormous one or involves an issue we feel strongly about. We then ask everyone to join hands.

"Join hands with the people around you. We don't need to form a circle. Just make sure that everyone's joined to at least two people." In a few instances a person will reach to the row behind and grab two hands together.

We normally do a short Bible study together. It's highly participatory. For instance, we talked about healing one night. I read a passage from Luke where Jesus healed a man. I spoke three or four minutes about healing and its implications for today.

"What about . . . ?" Nancy may ask.

Gary may reply. Or Shirley. Or I do.

We keep the mood informal. No one monopolizes but there's freedom to raise questions. Occasionally after the benediction small groups stand around and discuss the issues further. I encourage that.

\* \* \* \* \* \* \*

How did we evolve to that type of evening service?

In the late fall of 1974 an elder spoke up at a board meeting. "The only worship service we have is Sunday morning. Some of us are on shift work with rotating days off. We need a service on Sunday evening."

That gave us the impetus. But I asked, "Do you only want a duplicate of the morning service? Why not a different kind? A service where there's opportunity for participation . . . where we sing more . . . and have a variety of music."

The board agreed. Our first step was to use a piano for singing because I felt it lent itself to an informal setting. Personally, I feel it's easier to sing with a piano accompaniment.

We started our services with five or six songs, an offering, and a few minutes of congregational prayer, and then I usually taught or preached about fifteen minutes. After a few weeks, instead of my listing the needs for prayer, I began asking, "What kinds of concerns do you have? How about your requesting prayer?"

Several did. I included them in the prayer.

One Sunday evening I said, "Let's divide up the praying. You can be heard by Jesus Christ just as easily as I can. After someone voices a prayer request, I'm going to ask one of you to stop right then, lead us in praying for that request. Then we'll stop and go on to a second."

"I like that idea," Shirley said. "So often when I'm in church and the requests pile up, I forget one or two of them."

In our evening services at present, I stand in front of the people, but as concerns are shared, various ones raise their hands to express a willingness to pray.

It's been exciting for me to see that several of the quiet types are now praying audibly. One night Gary asked prayer for his father who's an invalid. June, who had never spoken in the service before, raised her hand. "I'd like to pray for that one."

Later she said, "I thought I'd never be able to pray out loud in public. But somehow it doesn't seem hard in this service."

Then came changes in our music. For instance, I taught them a simple chorus, "Yes, God Is Good," which we had sung often in Africa. But somehow the folks didn't make it sound quite right.

"You know, I think it's because the Africans sing with more than their voices. They inject their whole bodies and souls into their worship. They clap their hands. Some even more rhythmically or sway in place. I'm not asking you to be Africans, but perhaps you need the freedom to let go and sing this song with joyful abandonment."

We began again and I led them in clapping and singing.

Two weeks later we sang "Put Your Hand in the Hand" and someone started clapping as we sang. Now, clapping is frequently done on the happy, fast songs.

\* \* \* \* \* \*

Another feature of our Sunday evening is our prayer triads. It's not unusual to find groupings of three people talking and praying together on Sunday evening when we close our meetings.

Our triads started one Sunday evening when Thelma asked, "Why can't we have regular prayer partners? Someone we can talk to during the week when we need help, or when we want to share."

"Okay, why can't we?" I asked. "How many of you would like something of this sort?" Over half of the 60 people present raised their hands.

"Instead of having only one partner, I'm going to suggest we have two partners. These two people will pray for you every day. You, in turn, will promise to pray for the other two every day. How does that sound?"

That started our prayer partnerships. We decided to try it for a period of four Sundays.

"I'll lay down two rules. First, the agreement to pray for the others every single day. Second, as much as possible, meet with your partners every week. You can check in with each other and find out how the other's doing. Find out the areas where they need prayer."

Four Sundays later I said, "Let's see how the prayer triads worked. Do you want to keep on? Do you want to stop?"

"Oh, we can't stop!" Thelma said. "I've had such a wonderful time with my two partners. I hardly knew them before. Now we talk on the phone. We pray together. We have something to share with each other. I've learned to love my two new friends."

"Yes, that's exactly the way I feel," Donna said. "I'd like to change partners. The two I got this time will always be my close friends. I'm sure of that. But I'd like to have the same opportunity to know some other people as closely."

Those two were the most vocal, but everyone else agreed it was a good idea.

We have changed our methods slightly. In the beginning I simply said, "If you want to be part of a triad, raise your hand."

Then I quickly went across the congregation pairing up three people for each group.

Now we sign up for two months at a time. I keep a list posted on the hallway bulletin board.

Occasionally we have group-wide contracts. During December, for instance, we presented five areas of concern. A person could agree to pray daily for any or all of the five requested items. We covenanted to pray daily for a month. One was a monetary need, another centered on youth, one on our women's organization, and one centered on a need in our Sunday school. The major item was the need for at least one more man in the choir. By the end of January, all five items had been answered. That was the Sunday Jim Steele joined the choir. He may not have been aware that he was an answer to our prayers, but we knew!

Here's what a list looks like:

---

PRAYER PARTNERS

September and October, 1977

Rules

1. I promise to pray for my partners every day.
2. As much as possible, I'll make weekly contact with my partners.
3. I will pray daily for spiritual renewal for myself and for Riverdale Presbyterian Church.

_____   _____   _____

_____   _____   _____

_____   _____   _____

---

For those who are not members of our church—and we have several who have signed up—we ask them to pray for their own needs. We're not committed only to Riverdale Presbyterian Church. We want to spread the blessings everywhere.

Not everyone signs up. People are free *not* to participate. We want to offer love, concern, mutual sharing. We also want people to have the freedom to say, "Great idea, just not my thing."

We're learning that people care in all kinds of ways. Some can care by overt actions, like praying for others in group situations. We have compassionate people who care every bit as much but who find it difficult to discuss prayer and their needs. I know of one man who has committed himself to God to pray daily for several people, but hasn't told them. "I'm embarrassed to talk about prayer. I pray and I have a daily time with God. But I'm not able to talk about it." We don't want to push people into uncomfortable situations.

Last Sunday night after the meeting, Joe said, "It's great to go to a church and know that the people accept you just as you are."

Betty replied softly, "You know . . ." and then she paused as though the idea had suddenly hit her, "there's a lot of caring going on in our church." She paused again as the truth of her words seeped in, "There's a *lot* of caring."

# 9.
## they count, too

"Hey, let him go, it's my turn!"
"I got here first."
"But I've been waiting a long time."

Those words—plus a few more—I heard Sunday morning at the end of the worship service. Robyn, Lynn, Brant, and Brian, along with two others, started hugging me and not wanting to let me go. They didn't seem to mind that other people in church were leaving and wanted to greet me.

A minute later Philip hugged me and then David latched on and the three of us stood in a kind of huddle by the church door.

Crazy behavior? Not really. These are the children from our church. These are the kids who know I love them and that they are important to us at Riverdale Presbyterian Church.

We've always *said* we care about our children and believe in ministering to them. But do we really? Have we?

Those are the questions I've been asking myself. Of course, we have Sunday school, I said to myself. But how much more?

We give an occasional party or perhaps set up a few activities for them, but are children really significant in the life of the church?

Let the quality as well as the quantity of our activities for children tell the story of our theology. Theology really tells itself in what we do, more than in what we say.

That's one reason why I've been putting more and more emphasis upon the children of our church. In one sense, they are the leaders of tomorrow. But at the same time, they are the people of today: young, immature, but people. And that qualifies them for our attention and concern.

And one of my main areas is the children's sermon.

This provides the fun part of the service for me. At approximately 11:10 I announce the children's sermon and invite the youngsters to the front. They sit on the floor around me.

I do a five minute sermon, nearly always illustrated, and on the level children can understand. That means concepts within the grasp of children under 12 years of age and a vocabulary void of theological jargon.

I started doing children's sermons at Clifton Presbyterian Church. Most seminary graduates begin their ministry at a church like Clifton. Small. Mostly elderly members. Few or no children. Mine was no different except that my son, John Mark, was eight years old. Brian Bache was four.

Didn't those two have a right to hear the gospel in a way they could understand? That's the question that troubled me.

*But give a sermon for two people?* I argued with myself.

The answer shot back: Some of Jesus' best sermons involved a single person. Like the woman at the well.

*But are all those older people sitting there bored while I talk to the kids?*

Didn't Jesus say, "Permit the little children to come to me"?

I made my decision. I told the combined board of three elders and two deacons how I felt. I prepared several arguments to defend my position.

"Fine, Mr. Murphey, that's fine," said Hugh Hollingsworth.

"We feel children need the gospel, too," Emile answered.

So I began the children's sermon. In a few weeks we had four children in our church. Not long afterwards we had nine children coming regularly. They sat in the second row and I never heard anyone complain of their restlessness.

At my second parish I announced to the elders my plan. "I'd like to do a children's sermon every Sunday."

"Every Sunday?" an elder asked. But no one dissented.

That first Sunday I said, "I'd like all the children to come to the front. I have a special story for them." This being a larger church, about fifteen came forward. They listened. They answered my questions and then returned to their seats at the conclusion.

After the third Sunday, an elder called me aside. "Mr. Murphey, some of the people are complaining. They say you're wasting too much time in the service with those kids. I think they'd like to have you stop the children's sermon."

"I'm sorry they feel that way. I sure don't want to upset anyone. But don't you think we owe something to our children?"

A puzzled look creased his face. "Uh, oh, I guess so."

"What we've been saying by our attitude, if not by our words, is that children don't really count. God isn't interested in you until you become a teenager—except in Sunday school, of course. Don't you think we ought to let the children know we care? That they're special to us?"

He nodded. If not enthusiastically, at least he nodded.

Three Sundays later at the door he said, "You know, *I* enjoyed the children's sermon this morning. It was a lesson for me as well."

I smiled and thanked him.

Six months later he said, "I hope this won't hurt your feelings but sometimes I get more out of your children's sermons than I do the regular ones."

It didn't hurt my feelings. "I'm glad you're getting something out of the worship experience. I don't care if it's the hymns, the prayers, or the organ music, so long as you feel you've been ministered to."

When I first moved to Riverdale, I discussed the children's sermon with two parents. They didn't oppose the children's sermon. They only felt it would not be effective.

"We want our children to learn something. It's awfully boring for my five-year-old to sit through an hour of regular worship, and he's too small for the kindergarten."

We developed a compromise position. All children four years old and up are invited into the sanctuary. The children's sermon takes place about 11:10, after an opening prayer, the

Lord's Prayer, and a hymn. As the children's message concludes, all four- and five-year-olds go into our educational wing for a special forty-five minute program.

This begins teaching them what goes on during a worship service. From time to time the teachers explain what we've done during the first quarter hour. They're also told, "Just think, when you reach six, then you can sit in there with the others."

We considered the junior church idea of special services for all children through elementary grades. One day we may work on that concept. But I feel there's something wholesome and significant about families worshipping together. And even though the younger children are there only 15 minutes, it is a beginning. We're training them for the future because we care.

What about the results?

Every Sunday morning children greet me at the door. I receive effusive hugs from girls *and* boys. Almost every Sunday morning children come from the kindergarten room, around to the front door, and hug me before they'll get into the car.

I love those children—their expressions tell me they know it. Their actions also tell me that they care about me. And because we care, we're looking for ways to minister to the children.

Amuse-You-Tuesday began this past fall. It didn't come out of a great brainstorm in my office. It came about because of Vicki Turner.

"Cec, we've got to do something for our kids. Something more than we're doing now. The teens get a lot of attention, but what about the ten-year-olds?"

Hers was the first voice. Others followed. And I've learned that when I start hearing needs expressed, it's time to listen.

One Tuesday morning eight of us sat in an empty classroom. "What do we need to do to meet the needs of our children?" I asked.

After an hour of discussion we decided that our children needed an enthusiastic presentation, solid biblical content, and a certain amount of physical activity: drama, crafts or simple recreation. A fun time that also involved learning. We called it Amuse-You-Tuesday, a nonsense name, and the kids liked it.

On Tuesdays, we start at 4 P.M. For those who arrive early, fruit juice and a cookie await them. Occasionally, we start the hour with crafts and the children begin working on that immediately.

Normally I spent ten to fifteen minutes on singing. I'm not a great singer, and as the pianist has said to me a couple of times, "How can I find your key when you sing somewhere between two of them?"

But I am enthusiastic, and I can make the children sing. We do action songs. We learn Bible verses set to music. In six weeks we learned to sing all the books of the Old Testament.

Then I, or one of the volunteers, do a Bible story. Usually we rely on the flannelgraph board, or flashcard pictures, puppets, or chalk drawings.

Then two creative gals, Ellen and Marcia, combine crafts and physical activity. They either have the children dramatize the story they've heard, as when we did the three Hebrew children in the fiery furnace. Or they make 3-dimensional ravens out of construction paper, each with a piece of bread in its mouth to remind them that God sent the birds to feed Elijah.

We're trying to entertain—but more than that. We want to show that we care, that we really love them.

On Sunday evenings we have our Good News Club. Learning centers are set up around the room. One child might be listening to a cassette tape telling the story of Abraham leaving his country. Another child will view slides of what the country looked like in ancient Palestine. Three others are in a corner building a tent. Another group does simple research to find out what kind of food the patriarchs ate.

We're also considering other programs. For instance, at our monthly church family service, we're having a special program for children when we have adult speakers who really don't interest them. And we've talked about having the children handle the program at least once a year.

Jim, a gifted musician, is developing an unusual choir. Recently kindergarteners through sixth grade sang a psalm of praise while the teenagers followed in with "Day by Day" from *Godspell*. Since we have children who play diverse instruments as a French horn, clarinet, and guitars, Jim has even written them into the same musical number.

We're having outings and parties and probably a lot of the types of activities other churches have. Our membership is only three hundred, which shows that it doesn't take two thousand members to do these kinds of programs. And we're doing all these activities with one basic concept in mind: We want to show children that we care about them.

# 10.
## measuring up

"I had to share my good news with someone. Yours was the first name that popped into my head," Beckye said, "so I gave you a ring."

I enjoyed hearing a part of the good things going on in her life. She had recently been asked to teach the third-grade Sunday school class. "It's wonderful to feel I can do something for someone else."

Then she told of other activities in which she had become involved. "You know, this last year has been the happiest year of my whole life."

"Beckye, I'm glad that our church has been part of it."

"You know, I've changed. And Jim—he's really come out a lot. He's become open with people. More friendly. And both of us have so many wonderful things going on in our lives."

After Beckye hung up, I stretched back in my chair, propped my feet on my desk, and reflected on what's been happening around here in the past couple of years.

I know caring had been going on previously. It didn't start the day I became pastor. But it had begun in my own thinking six weeks before I moved to Riverdale. That's when I accepted the call as pastor. And I committed myself to spiritual renewal in my own life and in the life of my new congregation.

Part of this I've already described in chapter two. One result of that experience directed my line of praying. I prayed for the people of Riverdale Presbyterian Church and for the community every day. I asked for a spiritual awakening. I also asked something specific for myself: "Lord, make me a caring person."

After all, He made me know, even before the pulpit committee contacted me, that this time the direction was toward building up a loving, caring fellowship. It had come because I had prayed, "Lord, help me know *specifically* what you want."

Before Riverdale, I had preached at little Clifton Presbyterian Church. Located in a tucked-away pocket of the inner-city of Atlanta, many people don't even know it exists. People were discouraged, feeling isolated from other churches and even from themselves.

When elders from that church approached me and I consented to go there, I prayed specifically for guidance. "God, I know you want me to work hard. But you want more than hard work. Help me know what you want accomplished at Clifton . . . and specifically what you want accomplished through me."

*Hope.* That's the word that kept coming to me. Give them hope. Help them know they can be used. They're only 40 people but they can grow. They can minister in that community.

I went to Clifton while doing graduate work and stayed slightly over two years. We had all the problems of little churches: inadequate resources, not enough trained teachers, a continual struggle for money. But good things happened, too. New faces appeared, new activities. At the time I left, a Christian youth organization met in the church every Monday night. Nearly eighty high school students came. Our evening service consisted of about 30 people, with only one or two of them over forty. We saw that things could be done even by a small church. And people began to hope.

My second church had an active membership of 450 people. But the neighborhood had become transitional, from middle-class white to lower-middle-class black. They faced different problems than Clifton.

"We don't know what will happen."

"We don't know if integration is possible in the South."

"Can we hold a vibrant congregation in a declining community?"

We tried to minister to our own needs and to affect the people in our neighborhood. Three years later we closed as a white church and today a strong black Presbyterian church ministers in that area.

Then to Riverdale. Why does God want me in this particular church? That's a question every pastor needs to ask himself. And many reasons emerge immediately. To evangelize. To teach them more about Jesus Christ. To minister to people. To build up membership and resources. To preach edifying sermons. To do pastoral work. To visit the sick and shut-ins.

But *specifically?*

As the days moved forward, the sense of mission became clearer: Teach them to care.

During those first months in the new situation, I kept asking myself, "How can I become more effective? How can the church be more loving?" I'm still getting answers, still rethinking the original questions, still moving on toward a deeper commitment of myself *and* the church.

In this process I'm constantly trying to open myself to the Spirit's leading, trying to assess our effectiveness, trying to gauge our progress.

How do we go about measuring the level of love in a church? How can we devise an objective instrument that lets us know if we're doing a splendid job? Or only adequate? Or failing badly?

There is no answer for that one. However, there are *indicators* of the spiritual temperature of our church. Things that point out that we're becoming a congregation of caring people.

*First,* the gossip level.

Why do people gossip in the first place? Feelings of personal inadequacy? Jealousy? Even a matter of not liking themselves?

An eye-opening incident occurred a few years ago. I worked with two ministers in the same area. They happened to be related to each other. I liked Al—a warm person, always ready to go out of his way for a person. His brother-in-law, Marvin, was a pusher, hard-working, ever in a hurry. Always another battle to win.

One day someone mentioned Al's name in conversation, saying off-handedly how Al had hurt his own church. "He's just a pushover. Never takes a stand on anything. Whoever pushes hardest get's Al's backing. He really doesn't provide the leadership they need."

"I think you're awfully harsh on Al," I said. "He may be weak in exercising dynamic leadership, but that man has so much love shining through him."

The others agreed and we went on. A few minutes later I mentioned Marvin. "That guy's a tough one. Runs everything with an iron fist and—"

"Hey, wait a minute," said the fellow who had made the statement about Al. "You really knocked me out of the saddle about Al—and that's okay, because I shouldn't have said it. But now you're doing it to Marvin. And, oddly enough, he's one of my close friends. I don't like to hear people say those things about him."

I laughed. And as the irony struck me I laughed louder.

I had learned another lesson—the hard way perhaps—but a lesson. I had loved Al, and so I could defend him. But Marvin, not one of my favorite people, received the brunt of my sarcastic, slurring remarks. I didn't even feel a twinge of conscience. He just wasn't very important to me or to my personal world. But Al—a different matter entirely.

That's part of what I've learned about backbiting and whispering. People we care about—really care about—don't get chewed up and spit out. They get protected. We're not blind to faults, but we understand rather than give private or public criticism.

That's one thing I've noticed declining in our church.

*Second,* the rumble-grumble level.

Like hearing, "Nobody wants to do anything around here."

Or, "With all these new people coming into the church, I sure wish they'd get involved and do something."

Then to hear only minutes later in another section of the building, "What kind of a church is this? You ask an older member to work on a committee and you get an answer like,

'I did my share. Let someone else have a chance.' And I guess we new people have to carry the load."

Those attitudes and words tear down a church. An attitude of grumbling and rumbling and seeing only the dark side of everything. Or always looking backwards at what the church used to be. Or dreaming of what the church ought to be.

Like Herman, a 52-year-old, second-generation member. He said to me, "I don't even feel at home in my own church anymore. I've given my life here and now I hardly know anyone. I don't like the changes and I feel out of place."

Some of that still takes place. But I'm hearing less of those complaints all the time. When real caring takes place, people eagerly work together. Older members, knowing they're still part of the team, flow with the changes.

But what about the positive signs?

Churches easily get caught up in the "numbers racket." The size of their attendance or the amount of their giving measures their spirituality. Or do they?

At one church I pastored, we had one of the highest per capita giving figures for any church in our area. What the figures *didn't* show was that most of this high giving came from two families.

Attendance does indicate interest, no question. The growth (or lack of growth) may indicate what's going on. But I'm reluctant to equate size or growth rate with caring.

We have had numerical growth, from an average attendance of 100 people to twice that much. That led to folding chairs in front and sometimes in the aisles. We now regularly have two morning services. But those are not, at least for me, the real indicators of caring taking place.

But there are several *people* indicators!

The Bridge Builders held a lunch-after-Sunday-morning-worship-class-meeting. Suzie spoke up. "Let's all join hands as we pray for our food and let's thank God that we're here today."

What's unusual about that? A year ago Suzie wasn't sure she believed in prayer. She surely didn't talk about the subject openly. And joining hands? Not that gal—she wanted to keep her distance.

Or Arnie who left our church for another and stayed there nearly a year. He returned and said, "I can't put my finger on it, but something's happened here, I feel more a part of this church than I ever did before. Or... is it because I've changed?"

Both could be possible!

Other people indicators—When you walk into the monthly meeting of the Men of the Church and get a hug. When a husband and wife say, "Jesus Christ has become meaningful in our lives and the people here have made Him real."

When a man gets a chance for a job advancement 600 miles away and turns it down "Because I believe the Lord wants me to stay here and grow. I can change jobs next year or get a promotion another day."

When the minister's wife undergoes emergency surgery and two people come up to spend the waiting time with her husband. And a dozen others form an emergency prayer chain.

When two women who've never been very much involved in any projects or programs say, "This is fun. It's not a burden helping these people, is it? I'm so glad I have the chance."

When people say, "I felt something special at your church." Does it matter if they can't define the "something"?

I don't have objective, impersonal means of evaluating a caring church.

But then... I'm not sure I want impersonal, objective means.

Christianity means Jesus Christ caring *for* people *through* people. How can we possibly measure that? Or do we even want to? Why depersonalize self-giving? Or spend hours analyzing openness and change?

We can set up programs and projects out of a concern, but the real answer about effectiveness comes out in the personal lives and testimonials of those who have come into contact with us.

My measurements may be inaccurate, but that doesn't trouble me. I feel loved and cared for. A number of other people in this church have those same kind of feelings. That's good enough for me!

# 11.
## but not for everyone

"I just don't like your services at Riverdale Presbyterian Church," Jim said. "I let you come over here and visit me because I wanted to tell you how I felt and that I don't intend to come back. And that I'm not interested in hearing from you again."

The words came softly and I didn't feel he had unleashed a lot of venom. He only wanted to make it clear where he stood.

"Okay. We have a style of worship at our church that obviously doesn't meet everyone's needs."

"I don't go to church to make a lot of friends. I've got plenty of friends. I go to church to get away from people. I want to sit in the sanctuary and meditate and hear words of encouragement on how to live a better life. But I'm not interested in that mixing together and all that buddy-buddy stuff."

"Fine, Jim. That's your privilege and I hope you find a church where you'll be happy."

I meant those words. I've learned to accept—at least most of the time—that some people don't respond to our style of worship.

At the same time, I want to like everyone. I want everyone to be my friend. But realism says that's not possible. I turn some people off.

"The church has lost some of its dignity since you came," one maiden lady said.

One young couple visited our church and later told one of our members, "It was noisy—like a sideshow or something. We like the quiet worship and sense of serenity that comes along with it."

Fred expressed it in a more roundabout way. "You're pulling for a kind of *commitment* I'm not able to make. We like going to church. We like you and the people. But I'm involved in medical research. My work prevents us from living like normal people and having the normal type of social and religious activities."

Perhaps the remark of one man who didn't respond to our church said it best: "I don't want to get intimate. I'm a very private person."

That's how it goes. Everyone doesn't respond to our style.

They give me a number of reasons. I think there are others which, while valid, aren't mentioned. Or perhaps people aren't aware of them.

One of them is *distance*. Maintaining a physical and emotional distance is important for some people. They operate best with a desk between them and those with whom they talk. Some preachers are most effective with a pulpit between themselves and the congregation.

Rick and I went through seminary together. While not really close friends (I don't think Rick had any close friends), I had always felt sorry for him. Unmarried and from a broken home, during the holiday periods he stayed in the seminary dormitory. He ate his meals at a local cafeteria. He slept a lot or listened to music alone in his room.

When Shirley and I found out, we invited him to several meals during each holiday season. Rick never opened up and became our close friend.

After graduation from seminary, we didn't see Rick again for several years. One evening another minister called and said, "Hey, Rick's in town and he's staying overnight with us. How about you and Shirley coming for dinner? We can have an old-acquaintance time."

As we walked in the door, I spotted Rick coming toward me. Impulsively, I hugged him.

He backed away, obviously embarrassed.

During the evening I noticed that Rick never sat close to anyone, not even his wife. When talking, he seemed more comfortable being in one corner while the rest of us bunched together in chairs and the sofa.

I accept that about Rick. He's more obvious than many others, but he has helped me be more aware that some people need to keep their distance.

*Second,* some people are afraid of intimacy.

Bud talked to me one evening until the early morning hours. Depressed, his job in jeopardy, he had made several simple but unwise decisions.

"I've just not been able to talk about this to anyone," he said. Then Bud buried his head and for several minutes he wept. Twice he tried to calm himself long enough to apologize, but he didn't make it. The tears flowed again.

Finally I said, "Go ahead and cry. I'll wait until you've finished. And I'm not embarrassed."

After he had calmed down he said, "You're the first person I've opened up to in twenty-three years."

"That's a long time to keep everything bottled up inside."

"I had a friend once, Lenny. We could tell each other anything. But I made a mistake. I told him some things because he was my friend. I found out later that he told at least two other people."

"And that hurt you very much?"

"So much that I determined never to open myself up again. I wasn't going to be hurt again."

And now, nearly forty years old, he was falling apart, afraid, unable to let go with another person. After so many years, change may be very hard. Bud will probably remain somewhat afraid of intimacy.

*Third,* some are basically more reserved people. They've been conditioned that way through their life experiences. Opening up to others takes time.

Terry and I have known each other six years. It's taken that long for us to reach the stage of friendship. I was his pastor, but certainly not close enough for the label of friend.

But that's changed in the past few months.

We were drinking foul-tasting coffee from the hospital machine at midnight. Terry had been at the hospital since late that afternoon for an emergency appendectomy for his three-year-old daughter. Terry's former wife, now remarried, had breezed into the hospital shortly before nine o'clock and received the medical report that the child would probably be fine. As she scurried out, she said, "Call me if there's any further news. Or if you want me for anything."

We sat in silence, sipping the dark liquid. I was wondering if I ought to throw mine out and try it with extra sugar and extra milk instead of black. We must have gotten the dregs from a long day's coffee making.

Terry kept fumbling with his cup, sipping a little, putting it down, moving the paper cup around the table.

Finally he said, "I've never had a friend. Not a real one."

I nodded, not sure what to say.

"I don't know where to begin. I want friends, but maybe I'm afraid of people. Afraid that when they get to know me . . ."

"That they won't like you?"

He nodded. "Yeah, I guess it's like that."

"So you think people won't care enough?"

I don't remember all the conversation that followed. He told me that originally he came regularly to our church because of his child. "When you shake hands in the service, I always want to hide. I shake hands and smile if someone reaches over toward me. But I never do it first, not even now. I am learning to respond so that it's not so hard for me to smile back."

I think Terry's going to cross that barrier. But everyone isn't.

Wayne's never said this in words, but I sense he's absolutely unable to let down his guard. He never responds to a direct question about himself or his feelings. A neighbor said, "I've known that man for twelve years. He'll do anything to help anyone, but he's not close to anybody. No one knows how he feels about anything or what he's thinking."

Or Bill who said, "If I really told you about myself it would probably tear me up. I can cope by holding it all inside. That's the way I want to keep it."

*Fourth,* some respond to different stimuli.

Marty's a sports fan—anything from bowling to tennis to horseshoes. Mac, on the other hand, receives his most pleasurable moments listening to classical music. One man isn't superior to the other—only different.

"I've been a Baptist all my life," Sidney said, "and I like a lot of things at your church. But you wear a robe and you always pray the Lord's prayer—*every single Sunday.* I just find that awfully hard to warm up to."

The Stocktons visited our church three Sundays in a row. Then they began visiting another church. I met him on the street one day. "I like you very much and you're easy to listen to," he said. "But, well, it's just not the kind of preaching I'm used to or want."

"Oh?" I asked, not sure what he meant.

"You just . . . just kind of talk to us . . . and I want someone who'll really lay it on us. That's what I think of as real preaching. You're too easy on us."

Some folks, whatever their reason, use more subtle means to remain aloof. Take Agnes the clown. Start serious talk and she replies with a sharp retort, an affected manner, or says in her best Greta Garbo voice, "I vant to be alone." Funny lines. She's always doing stunts that get people's applause. But don't talk seriously with Agnes. She'll twist it around to humor again. One time in an informal setting she did a passable imitation of Edward G. Robinson with mannerisms, and said, "Now, listen, you punks, just leave me alone. Leave me alone, you hear." Then she moved away from the group.

Of course, there are reasons other than basic personality, fear, or training that keep people from responding warmly or becoming involved. What I'm learning is that I can also accept people who do not choose to respond. They're "okay" people. I don't want to judge their hearts or measure their spiritual temperature. Instead I can judge my own spiritual temperature by my acceptance of them, regardless of their attitude.

It's now a comfortable feeling for me (that hasn't always been the case) to acknowledge that everyone doesn't have the same kind of hunger. My task is to help motivate that desire and to channel it when a person does respond.

# 12.
## caring means *doing*

During my fourth year in Kenya, our missionary organization reached a crisis. Crises weren't new, but some pressed heavier than others. This time we desperately needed a temporary teacher in the boys' high school at Bukuria Mission, until someone could be recruited and sent out from the states.

"You could do it, Cec. After all, you have the educational qualifications. You've taught in the public schools and on a college level."

"I could do it, all right," I answered. "But I'm not going to."

"But, why?" David asked. "We've got to have help."

"First, I don't have time. I'm working with nearly four hundred churches. Training courses for lay preachers increasingly demand more of my time. I also know that if I take this job—even if it's only on a temporary agreement—I'll be stuck. Maybe for years." I had known that to happen with other mission groups.

"Aw, come on. A year at most . . ."

"But that's not the main reason. Frankly, I didn't come seven thousand miles to teach history and English. I came to teach people about Jesus Christ."

I held a very limited view of the Christian gospel in those days. Some missionaries felt called to teach, others to do administrative work, or medical work. The Quakers and Mennonites supplied missionary personnel to teach better farming methods. But I could see only one thing—the oral proclamation of the gospel.

Wisdom sometimes comes with age. I've been learning more and more the narrowness of my former position. It's the combination of *word* and *action* that really makes our testimony effective.

I should have seen that. I often wrote home to churches asking them to send their used clothes which I distributed to pastors and their families. We drove people with emergency-type illness over rutted roads to the nearest hospital. Shirley ran a small midwifery service, handling cases of troublesome childbirth. Our list increased in what we might call "social action" but we never thought of our activities that way. We saw needs and did what we could to provide for them.

And yet . . . when anyone mentioned ministering through other means or the words "social gospel" came up, I was the first to object.

"No watered-down message," I said. "We have to speak up for what we believe. We're not delivering CARE packages or substituting for UNICEF. Let's not get ensnared into becoming public service agencies and miss out on giving them the most important thing in the world—the word of salvation."

Despite that honest stand, I knew that the New Testament abounds with exhortations to help those in need. First John 3:17–18 occasionally troubled me:

> But if any one has the world's goods and sees his brother in need, yet closes his heart against him, how does God's love abide in him? Little children, let us not love in word or speech but in deed and in truth.

Of course, I had responded to actions which involved caring. But I had not consciously put together in my head that caring could also involve social undertakings.

As a person who has studied church history, I ought to have grasped that fact. John Wesley and George Whitefield set up orphanages. Hospitals and schools started in most nations as Christian incentives. In foreign lands missionaries had to teach people to read and write before they could do an effective job of communicating to them the good news.

I've wised up through the years. I still don't march in protests or wear a black armband or preach political directives. I didn't speak out from the pulpit specifically against My Lai or Watergate. But I do have a rising "social conscience."

At last, after twenty years of following Jesus Christ, I've become convinced that word and deed must march side by side.

As I learn, I'm teaching members in our church ways of showing people that we care, that we're willing to be inconvenienced and involved in other lives.

Mrs. Mickey Williams has helped me.

"Now listen, Angel Darling," she purrs over the phone, "this family was burned out yesterday. I've been around to furniture stores and the Good Will. I've pretty well taken care of things like that. The father's been out of work, but we found him a job starting Tuesday . . ."

Mickey has called so often in the past two years, I wait for the last sentence.

"And so all I need from Riverdale Presbyterian Church is fifty dollars."

"Mickey, I already have the checkbook on my desk. While you've been sweetening me up, I've filled in everything but the amount. I'm writing that in now. Come over and get it."

"See! I've been telling everyone that you're an angel!"

"Mickey, we're glad to help. We've not had to refuse any request so far that you've made. The folks here want to help."

"Yes, I know that."

And they do. In the past two years, they've shown that wonderful caring spirit. In my office hangs a framed plaque which reads:

HUMANITARIAN AWARD OF MERIT
October 1975

This award is given to Reverend Cecil Murphey and the members of the Riverdale Presbyterian Church by the Clayton County Economic Opportunity, Inc., for their outstanding service and contribution for the well being of their fellow man.

The E.O.A., a federally funded organization, helps people in emergency situations. They verify the claims and ascertain the extent of needs. They provide legal assistance, job placement, on-the-job-training programs, and a myriad of services to the elderly and handicapped. But their grants from the government don't begin to meet all the financial demands.

Our church is near the top of their list to call on for additional assistance. Perhaps they need $60.00 to keep the family's heat on. Or $35 to make the rent payment.

Sometimes Mickey asks for help for a client (never a *patient* or a *case*), and then adds, "Maybe you might visit the family." That's her way of saying, "I've sensed spiritual needs. See what you can do for them."

I paused from my writing after that last paragraph. Names and faces fly through my mind. I've enjoyed several wonderful experiences calling on those families.

Like Nora. Seriously ill, married to an alcoholic husband, she couldn't work and couldn't make payments on their two-bedroom trailer. Mickey handed her a food voucher, raided our church food pantry, and then we donated $87.00 for one month's mortgage note.

Later, Nora started attending our church. She's healthier now than she's been in a long time and holds down a good-paying job. "Mr. Murphey, you people came to me when I was desperate. I didn't think anyone cared. One preacher knocked at my door. I started telling him how awful everything was. He hinted that if I joined his church, they might help me. He kept saying that I needed to get right with God and then God would take care of my problems."

Nora dabbed her moist eyes as she continued. "You didn't treat me like that. You didn't even ask me about God until you'd done everything else you could. You cared about *me*. That's something I'll never forget."

As she talked I wondered how many times in the past I had given that same kind of impression that the other preacher had projected. Now I could praise the Lord that I came to Nora out of concern for Nora. Her attendance at our church was almost anti-climactic.

We're learning valuable lessons about caring. We're trying to put people and their needs first. We're trying not to ask, "If we help, will they join our church?"

Jesus didn't heal only people who recited the Ten Commandments or promised to join the local synagogue. He healed bodies, forgave sins, and delivered the bedeviled minds. Then *they* said, "Lord, I'll follow you wherever you go."

I'm discovering that other churches are awakening to the needy world around them.

For example, the Sunset Church of Portland, Oregon, holds a Thanksgiving service every year for those without families. Members provide the food and a family atmosphere.

The Eastside Baptist Church is located less than a mile from our local hospital and another mile from an inter-state highway. That church provides a wide range of services for the community, by working through the hospital.

Here's a partial list of services they offer: (1) someone to sit with individuals when the need arises; (2) care for children when one parent is hospitalized and the other needs to be at the hospital; (3) food for families and in some cases shelter in homes or motels; (4) transportation back and forth to the hospital or airport; (5) clothing when need arises; (6) washing clothing for persons in the hospital; (7) writing cards or letters to notify relatives.

Many churches operate day care centers and some have a "Mother's Day Out" when mothers in the community may leave their children, free of charge, in the nursery for a full morning.

In metro Atlanta where racial transition has been a long-standing problem, a group called the Ecumenical Community Ministry has been established. Several churches are working through federal, private, and religious agencies with the problem of "housing and related social services for low-income residents."

One of their first actions has been to acquire and rehabilitate houses in an older section of Atlanta. The houses are then sold to low income families.

One of our best resources for caring at Riverdale Presbyterian is our "Hunger Fund." The Sunday night offering goes into this account and I write the checks. Before the offering is given I announce, "This money goes toward meeting the needs of people in our own church as well as those in our community."

The amount collected averages about $30.00 a week. During 1976 (our second year with this account), we gave out over a thousand dollars to deserving people, most of that amount for people outside our church. Not a large amount, agreed. But in 1974, our records show that we gave out only $10.00!

We also ask members to bring non-perishable foods and canned goods for our food pantry. They respond beautifully. When we became aware that peanut butter was a high item for needy families with children, we were inundated with jars and containers of peanut butter.

Our folks regularly bring in used clothing. I sort through the clothes first because I personally pack a monthly box for nationals in East Africa. Members of an adult Sunday school class pay the postage. The rest of the used clothes go either to our denomination-sponsored orphanage or to the E.O.A.'s emergency clothing center.

Another Sunday school class discovered that people on food stamps could buy only edible items. So they try to purchase one carton of toilet paper a month. Another class buys soap powders by the case.

Martha Powell is now completing her second year as president of the Women of the Church. She not only does volunteer work at the local hospital, but has recruited and encouraged other members to do the same. She's gotten several members involved with a local nursing home.

Recently I chatted with the social director of the nursing home. "Those bibs! You don't know how much we appreciate them! The women from your church made 85 of them. These older folks really need items like this. And that nice Mrs. Henne comes over and reads to some of the ladies."

Then she added, "People forget the elderly so easily."

We're trying to remember them. And a lot of other people, too.

# 13.
## after they join

Rena joined our church. She really should have stayed at her former church. She probably would have except for one main reason.

"I got sick during the Christmas vacation and missed two Sundays. Not a single person from the church contacted me. Not even from the Sunday school, and I was one of the most active members. When January came I managed to limp back to school to teach my third-graders. I had spent most of my evenings and weekends in bed. I had gotten some kind of virus and just couldn't seem to throw it—lowgrade fevers and then sudden chills and a terrible headache all the time."

"No one visited me. For two years now I've not gone to that church and not a single person has called, written, or visited. I realize I have the responsibility for my own faithfulness. And I didn't expect people to come running to me every time I missed church—which wasn't often. But it hurt. It really hurt, as though no one cared about me. I wanted a church where I belonged to the fellowship."

She began visiting other churches. One day she worshipped at Riverdale and within a week I had seen her at her home. She's now an active member, but it's a real loss for her former church.

That's one way people respond to missing members: silence.

Or perhaps they actually wonder. They ask other members, "Haven't seen Rena lately. What's the story—do you know?"

"No, haven't heard from her."

"Someone said they thought she was visiting another church."

I've overheard conversations like that before. No one verifies. No one checks out the factuality.

Apparently a lot of people slip back outside the church after joining, largely because of neglect.

I'm not foolproof on following up on people. But I try to watch for those who miss several Sundays, especially those who normally attend regularly or involve themselves in activities.

I have several ways of following up on people.

*The phone.* A simple call that finds me saying, ı've missed you the past few Sundays. And I wanted you to know that I have missed you. I just called to find out if there's been sickness or if something's wrong."

Early in the conversation, I try to say something to the effect that they don't have to explain their absence. After all, I'm no truant officer. Jesus Christ didn't call me to be keeper of the attendance records. I want to let them know I've missed them—which means that I care.

How do I respond when someone in the church asks, "What's happened to Marty?"

If I know I answer, and then add, "Why don't you give him a call? He might be glad to hear from you. Everyone needs to know he or she is missed." Often these folks follow through.

*A letter.* Frequently I write to those who've not been around in a while. If I know the people well, I try to make it humorous.

Here's a postal card I sent to a young couple:

> I'VE MISSED YOU.
> This is not a where-have-you-been? card
> but a
> I-care-about-you card.
>
>

**after they join**

## Or here's one I sent to a family I didn't know well.

Once upon a time there was a father,
                     a mother,
                            and two beautiful blue-eyed boys.
And we liked them.
          A whole lot.
                    and we thought they liked us, too.
They came to the Lord's House
              and worshiped with us on Sunday
                  and always went to Sunday school
                        and nearly always attended family night suppers
(especially because mother was such a good cook
                        and father liked to eat!)
and then....
         whosh!....
                 two months ago, a vacant spot.
So I've wondered.
            Did an earthquake take them away?
                        No, or I would have read about it.
           Have they taken a flight to Mars?
                        Probably too expensive.
               Did robbers steal their watches and clocks and
                    calendars so they couldn't tell the times
                    and days for church?
         Hmmmm, maybe that's what happened.
Actually...I don't know the reason.
            I do know that I've surely missed them
and because I don't know all the facts,
         I can't properly end this story.
I wish they'd come back
         and worship with us
and then I could write
             "And they all lived happily ever after."

Or on a half-sheet size letterhead I wrote:

---

That poor preacher.
    Sad.
        Discouraged.
            Standing at the front door every Sunday....
looking....
   searching
      eyes glued to the horizon....
                and you don't appear.
So hard for that preacher.
   He likes you.
      He misses you.
         And wouldn't you like to help that man?
            Tell you what---
The next time you come to church,
   you'll find him standing out in front
      waiting for you
        and
          here's the first thing you'll notice:

Won't you help me smile again?

---

*A personal visit.* I have one of my volunteers set up an appointment for me to visit. In my early ministry I had several sad experiences of catching people unprepared for a knock at the door.

There's one visit I'll always remember. I rang the bell, a head appeared momentarily at a window. Then a voice shouted, "Wait a minute." I noticed a large picture window to my right and could see people frantically scurrying around, picking up beer cans. I noticed the husband was throwing them under the sofa. He finally let me inside and offered me a chair.

During the whole conversation, he was uncomfortable. He had missed a beer can and it stood on the coffee table. His eyes kept straying to the beer can and I tried not to notice. It turned out to be an uneasy conversation. I wasn't troubled over his problem, but obviously he felt guilty and embarrassed. I never visited him again without calling first.

And I remember one Saturday morning at 11:30 I called on a young woman who had visited our church twice. After an interminable wait, she slowly pulled the door open, and with a robe pulled around her shoulders, her hair disheveled and no makeup, she said, "I just got up. Can't you come back another time, pastor?"

*Listening to the Inner Voice.* I'm learning to listen when a name bursts into my thoughts. That inner voice may be the Holy Spirit. It may be only a kind of intuition at work. Or perhaps an unconscious putting together of a few isolated pieces of conversation, body language, and expressed attitudes.

For example, one morning Tom's name popped into my thoughts. I like Tom and he's a great personal friend. Then I went on back to working. A few minutes later his name interrupted my thoughts a second time.

My mind wandered a bit and then I pulled it back to the array of papers on my desk. A few minutes later Tom's name hit me a third time.

I reached for the phone and dialed his number. After we greeted each other I said, "Tom, I'm not even sure why I'm calling you. I've had you on my mind this morning."

"I know why you called. I've been sitting here by the phone, wondering who to call."

And then he unloaded his problem. It was a good experience for both of us. He received relief from his burden and found someone who could listen and understand. It made me feel good to know that I had obeyed that Inner Voice.

I don't think I'm either particularly mystical or especially sensitive to the Holy Spirit. (I confess I admire people who are and wish I were more perceptive about things like that.) But I've learned to trust that Inner Voice, especially when a name keeps troubling me.

*Regular visits.* I don't want to be around just for the crisis periods of life. I want to be available to the people in my charge as a friend as well as a minister. When I first came to Riverdale,

I visited every member of the church within eight months (except one or two who made it clear that, for various reasons, they didn't want a visit). I still try to visit each family occasionally. This is a chance to say, "Hello, how are things going?"

Other churches have developed the "Under Shepherd Program" in which an elder or responsible person in the church takes the spiritual oversight for one family or possibly as many as six. These under shepherds then inform the pastor of any needs he ought to know about.

At Peace Lutheran Church, Decatur, Georgia, they have established a variation called "Care Zones." Instead of grouping people geographically as in most programs, this is by interest. Some Care Zones concentrate on Bible studies, another on social activities.

"They're responding to each other. That's more important than the specific activities involved," pastor Roger Frobe told me.

I've learned one thing about caring: You can't care as effectively from a distance and separated by long periods of time. My attempt to be available, I believe, helps build effective caring in our congregation.

# 14.
## when in doubt . . . hug 'em

Tod Andrews died early one April morning. Immediately after receiving the news I rushed to see his widow. Mable tried to talk, but her voice faltered and cracked. Gray eyes filled with tears.

Then Mable hugged me. I encircled her with my arms. For several minutes, no words passed between us. Finally she straightened up. With a handkerchief she dabbed her eyes. She said huskily, "Thank you . . . for being here."

As I relive that experience, I recall other scenes, times when words couldn't quite convey the depth of feeling.

Our home church held a farewell service for us when we left for Africa. One by one members came by and shook our hands. Suddenly Bernice hugged me tightly. "I want to tell you how much I love you and Shirley, but I can't find the words," she half-whispered and squeezed me again.

Last summer we concluded a church leaders' retreat. At our closing exercise, each one held a chunk of French bread, then went to every other person, individually, and took a piece from each other's bread. Then each pronounced a benediction upon the other: "The Lord bless you and keep you" or "May his Spirit always lead you."

During the two-day retreat I had felt especially close to Lamar. He and I had been in a prayer group for the two days and prayed together several times. As he started to speak to me, he stammered slightly and then impulsively hugged me. I thought to myself, "You've given me a beautiful benediction."

Incidents like this have made me realize the importance of human touch. In fact, I have a kind of motto. When I'm with people and words don't seem to convey all that needs to be said, then I try this approach: *When in doubt, hug 'em!*

It works. Not because it's premeditated. Not because it's a gimmick. It works because it's an expression of caring.

Physical touch conveys so much. By the mere touch of a hand we express love, happiness, anger, agitation. Ever have someone grab you by the arm in a menacing way? Or poke a forefinger against your chest?

I remember old Miss Irma Linder from my grade school days. When I got out of the line, she grabbed me by the scruff of my neck. I always got her message and she never said a word.

For years the behavioral scientists have been telling us that gestures are extensions of ourselves. Through physical movements we speak as much—or at times even more—than through the medium of words.

Shirley and I began dating during my military days. We often talked about the future. I had a sense of knowing that God had sent her into my life but I didn't want to rush anything. She was a friend, a good companion. We had wonderful times together. But love had not entered the picture.

One night we sat in a crowded Bible study in a chaplain's office. I came in late because I had been on duty. My officer in charge had given me an hour to attend. I knew I'd have to leave before it was over. As I sat there while the chaplain led the discussion, I glanced over at Shirley. Somehow in that moment I knew that I really loved her.

And how do you tell a woman, ten feet away, in a room with 30 other people you've suddenly discovered that you love her?

As the minutes ticked away, I knew it was getting closer to the time when I would have to return to duty. I got up from my chair. I had to pass Shirley. Impulsively I reached out and stroked her hair and kept walking.

One evening, at least fifteen years later, Shirley and I were having one of our intimate talks. She said, "I know when I first realized how much I loved you. We were in a Bible study at

Great Lakes. You had to leave early. As you walked out, you touched the back of my head. That's when I realized how deeply I felt."

The message had come across! Touch said what words had no opportunity to express.

The other day I visited a hospital room where a ten-year-old girl lay, heavily sedated. Only minutes before, the doctor had told the father the stark truth: the tumor was inoperable. As I walked in, he stretched out his hand to shake mine. He stopped midway and fell into my arms. He sobbed a long time before he could find a voice to speak again.

The Bible presents an amazing amount of information about the touch of the human hand. In the Old Testament offerings, the high priest laid his hands on the sacrificial animal, then confessed the sins of the people. By that action he symbolically transferred the guilt of the nation onto the lamb.

Elisha was called to the home of a young boy who had died. The prophet stretched himself out on top of the child, breathed into his mouth, and life returned.

The New Testament abounds with the stories of Jesus touching people. Can you imagine the furor when Jesus laid his hand on a leper? Leprosy was an incurable disease feared by the people. No normal person came close to a leper. In fact, when a leper approached other people, he or she had to cry out, "Unclean!" then quickly passed on as far away as possible.

But Jesus defied all customs. He reached out and physically touched a diseased man (Matthew 8: 1–3). The gospel accounts are filled with Jesus making physical contact with people, from healings to blessing little children.

In most churches, the ordination to the office of minister has always been effected by the laying on of human hands. Church officers usually go through a similar experience. New church members customarily receive "the right hand of fellowship."

Mere physical touch says, "You are one with us. We identify with you." Then we look at our sophisticated world and we're afraid to get too close to people. Afraid to touch. Afraid to open ourselves. We keep our distance and retreat inside. I'm not suggesting meaningless backslapping or senseless hugging or excuses for sexual seductions. But I advocate freedom—freedom to express care.

In my first pastorate a number of children in the neighborhood got to know me. Some of them attended our Sunday school. Meeting them on the street, it was not unusual for Dawn to hug me or Tom to grab me. One little pre-schooler jumped at me, encircled me with her arms, pulled me down to her level and said, "Give me some sugar!" and then waited for a kiss.

For me, touch symbolizes our attitudes. The more uptight a man is, the more his physical body shows it through limited gestures, lips that scarcely move and hands that never reach out. A woman sits stiffly or moves backward as you come closer to her. They're both afraid of physical contact.

Then I think of Jesus. Children sat on his lap. He laid his hands on them. He touched lepers, the blind, the lame—all kinds of people. His touch brought physical healing, but liberated the soul as well.

People need our touch. They need our liberating and caring expressions.

Remember the story of the Good Samaritan? A dying man lay by the roadside, but the religious Jews passed by, unwilling to touch him, unwilling to defile themselves. Then an alien, a Samaritan, appeared. He picked up the man, cleansed his wounds, and showed mercy. That's the ministry God calls us to —the ministry of touch. We do it symbolically when we talk about touching lives. But we also need to give others our physical touch.

I encounter people all the time. Sometimes we want to offer comfort but words seem inadequate. *But I can sometimes say it with a hug!*

\* \* \* \* \* \* \*

Magda didn't like me, but then, she didn't like a lot of people. She was sick a lot. If I visited, she complained because I stayed too long. Or she complained because I didn't stay long enough.

One day I sat in her house and she repeated her list of complaints. For once I had the good sense to let her rant and make no replies to her terribly unfair charges. Mostly, I suppose, I sat silent because there was no way to defend myself. She had determined my failure; nothing I could say would help.

After nearly fifty minutes I finally said, "Magda, you're pretty miserable, aren't you?"

Her mouth fell open and she stared at me. I saw her eyes narrowing and I had no idea what she was going to say next.

"No one really likes me, you know," she said softly. "Everyone likes my husband. He's Mr. Nice Man. People at church hardly ever speak to me. They treat me as though I don't exist."

And in that moment I saw the loneliness and the emptiness of Magda's life. *I hugged her.*

She didn't change—at least not outwardly. She still complained as loudly as ever. But *I* had changed—at least now I really cared. And she knew it, too!

I don't hug everybody. Every situation doesn't call for demonstration. But when I'm not sure, I go by my feelings. I hug when I feel I'd like to hug!

Shirley's caught on to this. Normally a reserved type, compared to me, she's always been hesitant about physical touch. But she's come a long way in the past few years.

For instance, recently she and I called on a family. We wanted to talk to them about Jesus Christ. The wife's mother, a member of an extremely conservative church, was visiting. She had made up her mind not to like us.

The call went well. The mother even spoke her convictions and both Shirley and I agreed with what she said. She appeared surprised at first. She expressed concern about her daughter and husband getting their lives straightened out.

As we stood up to leave, Shirley hugged the mother. And that mother who had prepared herself not to like us, later said, "Oh, that must be a wonderful church! I want you to go there every Sunday!"

Several chapters in this book were read by members of a Christian Writers' group to which I belong. One of the members is George, a young man who has been going through real trials. After he read an earlier draft of this chapter he wrote me a note that I'll always treasure:

> I remember so well those hugs you've given me along the way. When I sobbed, it moved your body, too. Somehow it seemed like God hugging me, loving me, calling me son —through you.

Touching may not be the answer to every problem—but it goes a long, long way!

# 15.
## pastors need people, too

I chuckled as I read the bumper stickers of the car in front of me. One read, "Heaven is more than a Fire Escape." Another stated, "Men of Distinction Prefer God." But the one that really caught my eye was plastered to the lefthand corner of the bumper. It said, "Do a Good Deed Today: Say Something Nice About Your Preacher."

I'm not sure what the person who originated the bumper sticker had in mind and certainly no idea of how the cream-colored Pontiac owner interpreted the message. But it made me think.

Preachers need love and kindness. They're human. They may have learned to disguise their pain or to smile when they'd like to cry, but they need their share of being cared for.

As a preacher, it took me years to realize that. I comforted the sick and quieted the distraught. You have a problem? Come to my office on Tuesday and let's talk about it. You're frightened about possible surgery? Let's stop right now and pray for God to give you peace.

But who ministers to the pastor? Putting *Rev.* before our names doesn't exempt us from feelings of inadequacy, loneliness, jealousy, discouragement. We have our financial problems and even our sexual adjustments. We need sleep and food and large doses of love—like all other humans.

Some churches have become aware of this. The United Methodists have a pastoral relations council. In many cases it has strengthened an otherwise discouraged pastor. In some instances the members of the council have turned into the church's gripe committee.

From October of 1973 through the spring of 1974 I went through a painful period in my life. After fighting to maintain a vibrant church in a racially changing community, our church closed its doors. I was without a pastoral charge for seven months.

During that time I felt terribly alone and full of pain. I experienced feelings of rejection, and of failure. Perhaps people reached out to me during that period; perhaps I didn't know how to respond to loving fellowship.

But I've learned how in the last year. Today I acknowledge that I'm human. I need people and their love.

On Sunday mornings, during our "congregation at prayer," I usually say something like this: "Please pray for me, your pastor. I need God's wisdom and your support."

When people attempt to communicate how helpful a message has been, or what my actions meant, I no longer play the humble Christian. I used to say, "Just thank the Lord. It's all his doings." Now I say, "Thank you." And then praise him for using me.

I don't want to cheat the Lord out of his place in all of this. But the Lord works through people. And I'm one of those people he works through. Now I try something quite different.

Rita said recently, "In the past two months, you have come to mean more to our family that we ever thought possible. We love you so much."

And I could say, "Thanks. I'm glad I could be part of your lives and could share in your problems. And I love you both, too."

Does that sound simple? It is for me—*now*. But a year ago? I didn't know how to respond. I've been learning slowly.

The people at Riverdale Presbyterian Church have been ministering to me in the past year. First, of course, I've opened the door. At times I've admitted when I didn't have all the answers. Or didn't know what to do. Or when I needed their support and prayers.

The Sunday evening attenders have done so much to affirm me. Earlier in this book I shared the incident of Richard's getting up and requesting prayer for me. A few weeks later, Bob stood up and prayed for me. Both times it gave me a warm feeling. They cared. And I knew it.

Recently the Men of our Church served breakfast to members of a cluster of Presbyterian churches. Afterwards, the workers were cleaning up in the kitchen and I went inside. "Don, Dave, Gary—and all the others, I really appreciate what a fine job you did in taking care of this breakfast."

And Dave said, "And we appreciate *you.*"

Shirley and I went through an experience in the early fall of 1976 that helped me respond to the congregation's care more than anything else. Shortly afterwards I tried to write it down. Here is a record of my reflections:

The word didn't hold the dread for me as it does for many. As a minister and a pastor, that word occurs often. *Cancer.*

But this time it came from the lips of my wife. That made it different. Now it had struck our home. My wife.

Events moved quickly that week. After a hysterectomy months before, we thought everything would be smooth from then on. Then lumps in Shirley's left breast. The prescribed medication dissolved the first two.

Then, seemingly overnight, a new tumor. This time, large, hard, and painful to the touch. Next a visit to her gynecologist and from there an appointment with a surgeon. Surgery was scheduled for the following Monday at Clayton General Hospital.

"We hope it's benign, but we can't be sure until we operate. You'll have to sign a form authorizing a mastectomy if necessary," the doctor had said.

Others had gone through this procedure. Others had survived. We had the added complication of knowing that Shirley's father had died young with cancer. Both an uncle and aunt had died within the past three years with cancer.

We didn't talk about her impending surgery or its aftereffects that day when she came home from the doctor. I hugged her and held her for a long time. As we released, I said, "Honey, let's pray and commit you to the Lord."

I can't remember anything about what I prayed except that I asked for peace in our hearts and a willingness to submit ourselves to him.

Shirley, obviously shaken from the news of surgery within the week, didn't pray aloud. She squeezed my hand tightly as I prayed. Then I held her in my arms for a long time, neither of us saying anything.

Two days later, we visited a terminal patient together in the local hospital. After we had both gotten into the car and I was getting ready to start the engine, she said, "It won't make any difference to you, will it?"

I reached over and took her hand. "Honey, I love you, and it won't make any difference."

She closed her eyes and nodded.

"Shirley, I love you. Maybe you just needed to hear me say it, but it won't make any difference to me, even if you have a mastectomy and come out lopsided."

"I guess I just needed to hear the words," she said, and moved her seat to an almost reclining level.

We talked several more minutes after that, affirming our love for each other. We made a fresh commitment to Jesus Christ as well.

Earlier that day I had done a lot of soul searching and praying. "Lord, this may be the beginning of giving Shirley up. I don't know what will happen." After twenty-two years of marriage I forced myself to think of what life might be like without my best friend.

I attended a meeting of hospital chaplains that noon. Afterwards, two of the other chaplains talked to me and I told them of our news. One of them stopped right in the hallway and prayed quietly for Shirley and for me. A few minutes later, Jim sat with me in my car and asked me for details.

Then I cried. For the first time I let out all the emotion and felt grateful for someone else to listen to me cry. I had found release.

"It's okay, Lord. Heal her if you will, take her if you want, or I'm willing to accept anything in between." I meant that. I was ready.

Sunday morning in church we prayed for Shirley, already checked in at the hospital ready for surgery the next morning. At our informal Sunday evening service, we had hardly gotten started before June stood up and said, "I think we ought to pray right now for Shirley."

And we did. We even joined hands with each other, signifying our unity in this request.

At the end of the service, several people hurriedly got together. One of them came over to me. "Cec, it's all settled," Donna said. "I'll be at the hospital in the morning to stay with you."

"Oh, Donna, I . . . I . . ."

"Don't tell me not to come."

"No, I was only trying to find words to say that I'm touched that you want to be there."

"And since we don't want a lot of people running in and out, I'll call Thelma as soon as we know anything."

I nodded, "That's beautiful."

"Thelma has set up a prayer chain and everyone will be praying for Shirley in the morning and will keep on until I call."

Later I went by the hospital and talked to Shirley a few minutes about events of the day. Then, before I left, we again talked about surgery the next morning.

"Our love has grown so much deeper already because of this," she said. And I realized that it had. We prayed together again and I went home. I slept well that night and so did Shirley.

The next morning Donna reached the hospital before I did. She joined Shirley and me as we prayed again before the attendant wheeled her out.

Minutes later I looked up at the tall figure in the doorway. "Oliver!"

Oliver Wood is a pastor of our denomination in the next

town. Over the last year he and I have grown very close. He had known of Shirley's surgery and had said he'd be praying for her.

"Hi, Cec," he said simply and came inside the room. He pulled up a chair and sat down. We talked for ten minutes and then I said, "Say, you've probably got other things to do. I sure appreciate your coming."

He looked startled. "I came to stay with you. I cleared everything off my calendar so I could be here with you today."

For the next hour, he, Donna, and I talked about Jesus Christ and had a peaceful, beautiful time of fellowship together. He stayed in the room until the doctor walked in and said, "She's in the recovery room. I waited until I got the lab report back. It's benign . . ."

After he left, I felt a sense of relief. And so thankful. But the news came almost anticlimactically. God had already given me peace and a spirit to accept anything that happened.

"Let's join hands in a prayer of thanksgiving," Donna said.

Afterwards Donna called Thelma who, in turn, called the others. Several people from the church dropped by and chatted with me briefly. My secretary said the phone rang almost continually with people asking, "How's Shirley?"

Now, weeks later, I'm reflecting on that experience. People ministered to me and to Shirley. The situation had been reversed. I had been unable to help myself. Others had been there —loving, caring, praying.

Shirley and I had received so much. I, the minister, had been ministered to by my own parishioners and by another pastor.

Thanks, Lord, that people care.

Another incident happened in the middle of that hospital scene. It involved Sam and Dot.

At 43, Dot knew she was dying of cancer. She spent her last three weeks in the intensive care unit of South Fulton Hospital, a fifteen-minute drive from Riverdale. I tried to see her as often as possible.

On the morning of Shirley's surgery, Sam called our office

and the secretary relayed the message to me: "Dot is not expected to live through today."

I looked at my watch—10:05. Shirley was just now going through the surgery. I felt my place was there at the hospital. But what about Sam? He needed me, too.

"Contact Frances and Martha," I called my secretary Sandy. "They've both been close to Dot. Ask if they can go to South Fulton right away."

As I sat in the room, I said silently, Lord, I believe we need a man to go there, too. Someone to speak to Sam. A man who can open up and who can pray with him. Please, Lord, tell me who to contact."

And my mind remained blank. I still felt someone else needed to go to South Fulton Hospital. Ten minutes later I looked up and Jim Hull stood in the doorway.

"Hi, I didn't know what time Shirley's surgery was scheduled so I dropped by now."

"Jim!" I almost shouted. "You're an answer to prayer!" I hugged the startled man, quickly told him the situation and then said, "Jim, can you go to South Fulton?"

"Sure," he said and seconds later I heard the elevator door open for him.

That afternoon the details came in. Jim reached the hospital shortly after 10:30. He explained to a nurse that he had been sent by the pastor to pray for Dot. He took Sam into the room with him and Jim had prayer with both of them. "I don't know how much she understood," he said. "She was slipping away and she was at peace."

Five minutes later Dot died. Jim talked some more with Sam and then left. At the door he met Frances and Martha who came to offer their sympathy and support.

And I had been able to stay at Clayton Hospital, awaiting word from the doctor. The people from our congregation had spread love and caring—first to me, but also to others in need.

I'm learning more and more how to put into practice the theological concept of "priesthood of believers." It means believers being ministers to each other, even to their pastor. And in the next chapter I'll share a few of those ways we've been learning to actualize our theology.

We're not making perfect marks in our attempts. But we're thankful when we see the response of appreciation by those we've been able to care for.

# 16.
## I'm single and alone

After identifying himself on the phone, George said, "I enjoyed reading an article of yours a couple of months ago in *Christianity Today*. I decided that if I ever got back to Atlanta again, I wanted to call you up and thank you."

"I appreciate your calling, George. It always makes an author feel good to know that people read his material and find it helpful."

We talked several minutes about the article. I sensed he wanted to prolong the conversation and he began talking about himself.

"I was a pastor in South Georgia, until two weeks ago. Now I'm back in metro Atlanta trying to relocate."

"As a pastor?"

He made no immediate reply and then when he did, the words came haltingly, "Uh, well, uh, I'm—not—I don't know . . ." I heard his voice break.

"My wife left me three weeks ago. One of the deacons in the church said to me, 'If you can't rule your own household, then you certainly can't rule the household of God either.' So I resigned and came back here. My parents live in this area."

After a few more words together, I invited him to come over to the office and join me for coffee. Half an hour later he arrived. We spent time together that day, and a second afternoon later that week.

I helped him make contacts. Eventually George became a counselor in a crisis center in another Georgia city.

I'm glad I was able to help George and to be sensitive to his need for a shoulder to cry on. And George came into our church. He became involved in our activities and even taught an adult Sunday school class for three months.

But George did something for me. He made me aware of a need. The need of the single person.

"Cec, the folks are great here. And they really accept me. But we need activities for singles, for people like me."

Another divorcee said later, "The church is really couple and family oriented. That's okay, but it sure leaves us singles feeling terribly alone."

Then we formed the S.O.U.P. group—Single, Obviously Unattached People.

"We need to be with other singles," Janie said.

"Unless you've been married and have lost that relationship, you really can't understand what we go through," Paula said.

They're not all divorcees. There's Jim, nearly forty, and never married. "I came close twice, but my business kept me on the road and it never worked out."

Or Randy who's twenty and plans to marry eventually. Or Dan. Or Janet.

But they have needs—needs peculiar to the single life.

"We don't want to find friendship by having to bar hop, either," one said.

Our S.O.U.P. group meets on Sunday evenings in a Scout Hut which is on our church property. They meet at approximately the same time as our evening worship because we have a nursery available.

Interestingly, at least three singles have opted for the evening service—one a divorcee-in-process and the other two single. I asked them if they didn't prefer a service for singles.

"We feel our needs are being met here. There's a lot of caring going on here and we're looked at as people, not as singles," Joe Ann said.

Churches are awakening to the needs of singles. Perhaps other pastors are having a George come up to them and say,

"Hey, I'm single and I'm alone. I need association with people who are in similar situations."

And other churches are responding to these needs in a variety of ways. The Hapeville Baptist Church has a Sunday school class called Twice Single, open to all who are single for the second time in life.

However, at North Avenue Presbyterian Church, Claire Underwood, the Director of Christian Education, decided against a class exclusively for singles. Instead, she's been persuading individuals to get involved in the total church program, from editing the church newsletter to ushering on Sunday morning.

Integrating single adults into the life of the church followed Claire's own experience as a single adult.

"After college I seemed to be getting to know fewer and fewer couples and families, and I didn't know any well. I joined the staff here and realized I did have things in common with wives and mothers and enjoyed being with them. The more I was in homes, the more I realized I felt a part of something much bigger than the world I had been in. I was a part of a big community where I was cared about. I realized that if I could do that, maybe I could help other singles have this kind of experience," she said.

Claire cancelled the single adult Sunday school class for those over 30 and helped these singles find a place in other adult classes. She also encouraged them to take part in the weekly church supper, called the Gathering, in which the entire church family meets each Wednesday for an informal dinner and then splits into small group sessions.

She then began to cut down on the number of singles "events" while she encouraged individuals to help out in all areas of the church's work.

"So often with the big groups, you're just running a dating service. That's fine, but ministry is much more than that," she said. Finally, she developed a system of small support groups in which four to eight persons meet regularly and share their experiences and problems.

At Riverdale we made a similar decision. Singles need exposure to others. They need to be part of the world in which they live. To separate them could intensify their sense of alienation and guilt.

"Being with the Bridge Builders Class" (a class of young adults, single and married) "has been good for me," one divorcee said. "I'm a person with them. I don't feel so guilty all the time. I'm not always fighting and churning inside about why my marriage failed. And I've been invited out as a third wheel twice in the last two months. That really helps me know that I'm part of the class."

\* \* \* \* \* \* \*

In November I spoke at a Parents Without Partners convention. Although warmly received by many of the conferees, I sensed some hostility.

Like a thirtyish man in a brown turtleneck. "Where was the church when I needed it?"

I could only reply that many times our churches have failed. I also said that some of us were trying to reach out toward singles.

A middle-aged widow spoke, "All my old friends shy away from me. They see me as a threat—someone who might take away their husbands."

"No one came to me when I was hurting," one sullen voice said.

I responded, "We're part of the church but also we're human beings. We know we've failed. But don't give up on us. We need you. If you divorcees and widows stay away from us, how can we know your pain?"

Later, several of us went into the restaurant for coffee and nearly an hour of conversation. Marie and I talked most of the time.

She had been widowed three months after nearly thirty years of a very happy marriage. Parents Without Partners had helped her at a time when she felt ready to give up on life.

"I'm glad I met you today, Mr. Murphey. I live in Riverdale

and I've thought about coming to your church several times. In fact, twice I drove up to the church and then didn't have enough courage to park the car and come inside. Sounds silly to you, maybe, but to me—well, I lost a lot more than my husband when he died. I lost my self-control, my sense of confidence. I'm getting it back now."

Before we parted she said, "I'll be at your church soon."

I smiled. As a preacher I've heard that statement four hundred and nine thousand times. And I suspect that all of them mean it at the time. But few follow through. I wouldn't have been surprised if Marie hadn't followed through.

The following Sunday morning a sandy-haired man entered the church. I introduced myself to him at the front door.

He smiled as he extended his hand, "I'm Richard Roley. Marie told me about you and the church. I thought I'd come and worship with you today."

Richard hasn't missed a Sunday since then. The following week Marie came and brought Barbara. Two Sundays later I met Jack and then Helen.

Two days later a phone call from Marie. "Cec, how about a Sunday school class for us singles?"

I explained how I felt about it and why we had been negative about the separatism before. She insisted.

"Look, Marie, try an adult class for awhile," I pleaded. "See if you can fit in. If you honestly don't feel part of it, then we'll give you singles a class. We want to see your needs met."

A week later she cornered me after church. "Think about the class again. We need our own time together. It's not the people's fault here. Everyone's kind. They're friendly and always making sure we're not left out. The trouble is ourselves. Just as soon as one of them says, 'My wife told me . . .' or 'My husband and I went . . .' we feel cut off. They can't help it. But when they talk like that I feel like half a couple. So do the other singles. That's not their fault. It's *our* problem."

"Marie, that's what I needed to hear. *Your* problem. Okay, I'll talk to the Sunday school superintendent and see what we can do about a teacher."

"We have our own teacher," she said and threw her head back in laughter. "In fact, we have two of them—Richard and Wanda!"

She winked and said, "Besides, Wanda and Becky have picked out the curriculum materials."

The following Sunday morning we provided a room for them. At Riverdale Presbyterian Church we're now using all the classroom space we have. A class of elderly ladies volunteered to vacate their room and meet in a corner of the sanctuary. As one of the ladies said, "At our age we can't do much to help other people. We're glad we can do this little thing for them."

So the class began. The first Sunday twelve singles attended. Two new ones came the following week. The third week they said, "We can't keep referring to ourselves only as the 'New Class' or the 'Singles Class.' Let's pick a name."

They now call themselves the "All Spares Class."

Their concern doesn't end with the class. They're also singles who care about other unattached people. Whenever anyone visits our church who's not married, I pass the name on to Marie. She calls and invites him or her expressly to the singles' activities.

Recently they announced a party in the apartment complex where Wanda lives. They called it a "Bring-your-own-Bible party" and had a turnout of nearly thirty people.

Once a month they have a covered dish lunch after Sunday service and invite singles to stay with them.

Marie's having a special Christmas party this year—only singles invited, people who haven't any family. "Christmas is no time to be alone," she said. "Christmas is a time for sharing. And we can make our own family just by being together."

We don't appeal to all the singles in our community, but we're trying.

Recently Wilma parked outside our church on a Saturday afternoon. Dave and Joyce were working on a Christmas play. She walked over to them. "I'm so lonely, I just want to talk to someone."

She's been attending our church regularly since then.

And there's Teresa. A married friend said, "You really ought to try that Presbyterian Church. I've heard they have activities there for single people."

We've even had a few referrals from the local mental health center. They have our telephone number and information about our singles' activities.

"Marie," I said one evening, "I've been married exactly one half of my life. It's been so long that I can't remember what it's like to be single. I can't do a lot for you and I can't really be one with you in your problems, but . . ."

"Wait a minute, preacher! You care. That's doing something. That's doing an awful lot."

# 17.
## sharing grief

*Death.*

That's an impersonal word until it intrudes into our own circle of life. Then it becomes highly personalized. We associate the word with names and faces.

Sometimes we strive to shake off the impact by mouthing euphemisms. "Harry's gone," or "Mother passed away," or "Ralph's no longer with us."

Even at funerals, some preachers have blunted the concept of death by saying, "Olive has only passed through the door into another room."

But no matter how we try to soften the language, the fact stares at us: *people die.* Not only strangers listed in the obituary section of the paper, but close friends. A mate. A parent.

And somehow, even in the midst of that pain and with an acute sense of loss, we who care not only want to express our feelings, we know we must. Often we fight the frustration of "I don't know what to say."

I've heard people admit, "I never go to funerals because I never know what to say." So they opt for doing nothing. And feel guilty. Later they encounter the griever and say, "I didn't go to the funeral. I . . . I just couldn't." And then the mourner must try to console the other, and in words of one sort or another to say, "It's okay."

I know of that happening recently. Betty's father died suddenly of a heart attack. Two weeks after the funeral, Betty's close friend Helen called. "I'm so sorry about your father. I should have called you earlier—"

"I needed you then, Helen. I don't need you now," and she hung up.

Betty's actions may have been rude but she was still hurting. And her friend passed up an opportunity to share her grief.

I have lost several people close to me. My father, my older brother, my mother-in-law, as well as several good friends. I have grieved for them. I'm also a pastor and have been with people as they go through these times of mourning.

Through these experiences I've learned that there are ways we can genuinely express care. Here are a few.

First, *say it.* We may find ourselves getting choked up or fighting back tears, but let the words come out. Even saying, "I don't know what to say," is superior to silence. It shows your involvement.

Mere words aren't going to heal, but they help. They express our attitude.

Second, *show your concern.*

Earlier in this book I discussed hugging people. That's meant a lot to me in grief situations—both as giver and receiver. Sometimes that's the best way to express our concern.

How about a potted plant that can remind a mourner of your reaching toward him or her? A card with a handwritten message that can be as simple as the one a friend received, "I love you. And I hurt because you're hurting."

As in a lot of churches, our women prepare meals for families during the grieving period. There are a handful of folks who go in and clean homes if needed. Sometimes we've given offerings from our hunger fund. Or we set up memorials to express our love.

Another thing a few of us have caught on to: from the death announcement through the funeral people almost smother the bereaved. But two days after the funeral, friends stop coming by and loneliness sets in. This is a time when they need emotional support. Two or three of our caring folks make it a point to visit on a weekly basis up to two months. It's a way of saying, "Your mate died, but you're still living."

Third, *express the reality*. Is death so hard to talk about? I know only that people who talked frankly to me in the situations where I was the grieving one ministered to me. They used words like *death, loss, sorrow*. Their conversations helped me say, "It's real. Dad's gone. We'll not see each other again."

As a mourner I'm becoming aware of how important it is to help people say that for themselves. Little things keep triggering memories. For at least a year after the death of my mother-in-law (who was also one of my closest friends), things happened that propelled her back into the present.

For example, Mom Brackett wore one dress I especially liked on her. A lightweight silky material, brown with large white polka dots. At least six months after her death, I was walking downtown in Atlanta and I saw a woman getting on a bus. She was wearing a brown dress that looked very similar to Mom's. Immediately I stepped up my pace and started to yell, "Mom! Mom!" And then I realized that couldn't be Mom. The dress wasn't really the same. She didn't look like Mom Brackett. My reaction wasn't very logical—but grieving emotions aren't logical.

Another time an editor called me two weeks after my father's death. We talked about writing a series of articles. After hanging up, I heard myself say, "Wait'll I tell Dad. He'll be so proud." But again, three seconds later a clearer voice inside my head said, "He's dead. Dad's dead."

I'm thankful for the people who helped me (even with its accompanying pain) to accept the finality of death.

Fourth, *listen*.

In my pastoral position, I've been aware that some people continue telling me the same things over and over. One elderly man kept repeating, "I promised Mona I wouldn't let her die in a hospital. I kept her here with me and she died in her own bed."

Almost every time I visited, he told me the same incident. The doctor and his three children had wanted the ailing wife to go into the hospital. "It'll be easier on you," they told him.

He always shook his head. "We've gone down the road this

far together. I guess we can make it a little bit longer together."

Every visit he told me the story again. Not that it bored me, but I often wondered why he kept telling me the same incident. Perhaps there's a magic number—like 37 times—that the story has to be verbalized before a catharsis takes place. Perhaps each time you speak of your loss, you chip away a little of the encrusted hurt around your heart.

Fifth, *respect the right of silence.* When my father died, I felt drained on the morning of the funeral. Dozens of people had asked questions such as "Was he sick long?" "How did he die?" The story had been related so often that it sounded like a recording in my head. *Oh, Lord, don't make me tell it again,* I prayed that morning.

While we sat, waiting for the funeral director to signal the time to start, a friend reached over and patted my hand. He nodded but said nothing. He didn't say a word the entire fifteen minutes we waited. But he was there. Having another person nearby who didn't demand conversation helped me. I could sink into my own thoughts and silently grieve without having to talk about it.

Sixth, *don't smother.* Ella lost her husband and for two months she didn't come back to church. She had been active before, vivacious, heavily involved in the Sunday school programs.

We kept in contact. I visited and called several times. So did others. When she did come back, she said, "Now I'm ready to get back into the world again. I've been so smothered by my close friends I wanted to hide from everyone. People kept trying to keep me from being lonely. They couldn't seem to realize I didn't need protection, only concern."

\* \* \* \* \* \* \*

People in grief situations don't remain in a single state of emotion—they're up and down. Grief doesn't permeate every moment. I've observed people whose mood swings from deep crying and moments later to a joyous, abandoned state of mind. Effective caring responds to those mood swings.

There's no single rule for sharing another's grief, except possibly one: be sensitive and caring.

The guidelines I've written don't apply only to death, either.

My writer-friend Gary read an earlier draft of this chapter. He commented, "After my divorce, I kept going through some of those same things you mentioned about death. When you wrote about memories of your mother-in-law, I sure understood that. For weeks after my divorce I'd see a woman walking down the street. Her dress or her hair—maybe just the way she walked—reminded me of Linda. That went on for nearly a year."

He also told me that a married couple practically had him move into their home for two months. "I don't know how I would have made it without them."

Caring people respond to grief situations—death, divorce, which is a form of death—or any serious trauma. Caring people intuitively respond and their response seems to be appropriate. They know when to speak, when to remain silent, when to show concern.

Being a congregation of caring people in the midst of death and dying is no easy task. But that's one of the finest opportunities for us, the disciples of Jesus Christ, to say, "We love you. We stand with you."

# 18.
## caring through fun and fellowship

"You're not having any coffee," I said. "Let me get you a cup. What do you want in it?"

She shook her head. "I don't really like coffee."

"Juice then? We've only got orange today. How about a glazed donut?"

She shook her head again. "Actually, I've had breakfast. I'm not hungry or thirsty. The noise sounded so delightful in here I just wanted to stop in and listen."

"You can't do that," I said. "You also have to mingle." And before she could say anything more, I had taken her hand and led her over to three women chatting about carpeting one of the classrooms. "I'm not sure if you know Carol Wheeler. She attends the Covenant class occasionally."

"Hi, I'm Becky Tindell . . ."

I left the group and went on to someone else.

That's how our Continental Breakfast works. We provide coffee and pastry in our fellowship hall prior to Sunday school. We place a can on a table with a sign FEED ME, TOO. We always lose money because contributions never quite cover the expense. But we're not as concerned about the profit or loss as we are about fellowship. About people getting acquainted. About people getting to know and appreciate each other.

We've even run this ad in the church announcements page of a local newspaper:

We try to make our ads person-centered. Instead of telling how wonderful our singing is, the greatness of our preaching, and the range of our programs, topping it off with a picture of a preacher's frowning face, we take an entirely different approach.

We try to make our ads speak to the people's needs. Like

\* \* \* \* \* \* \*

We're trying to show people in our community that we're interested in them. We're just as interested in our members. Having fun together also expresses that caring.

"Unless you've got something you want to change," Marcia said uncertainly. "I mean . . . we don't want to run things. . . ."

"No problem there," I assured her. Your ideas excite me and I want to encourage you in pursuing them."

Her dark eyes lit up. I knew Marcia needed those words to get even more involved with the new group.

They call themselves the FUNdamentals. Their whole purpose for existence centers around fun activities—but activities that involve the whole church.

"A-caroling-we-will-go" became their first project since the committee formed itself in mid-November. They scheduled caroling at eleven homes of elderly people, presenting the shut-ins with small baskets of candy. Refreshments were served later for the singers. Fifty-two people went caroling. One group

caring through fun and fellowship

followed Jim, who led them by playing his guitar, and Suzie led the second group with her guitar.

What came next? An original play written by two members of the church. An all-church skating party. A night of simple games and fun time at the church.

In February, the FUNdamentals organized a church-wide talent show called "Some Stars Are Born." Both Sunday school classes and individuals signed up.

The response amazed us! Every class in the church responded. Two different children played the piano. One sixth-grade girl presented her tumbling routine, a teen-aged boy played guitar. The adults weren't left out. Barry and Denise did a pantomine. The Joy class (13 middle-aged adults) recited Ogden Nash poetry. The singles class sang two musical numbers and Bob sang "The Impossible Dream." Even Shirley and I participated in performing an original skit. Mae Cook, who is ninety-one, wrote a humorous poem and, unable to attend, recorded it on tape.

What's ahead? They've just completed an organized Easter egg hunt with a costumed (and home-made costume, too!) bunny helping the younger children. We now have organized softball teams for men and women.

They're trying to help us and others know that Christians have fun. And that we can learn to know and care about each other even in the middle of those fun activities.

\* \* \* \* \* \* \*

I've not devoted any space to our youth programs. As I've talked to pastors and visited other churches, this area has received a wide amount of attention and effort. It's the one area where I've felt most churches do a fairly good job.

At Riverdale we have a growing youth group sparked by two volunteers, Judi and Bill. They work toward teaching our youth about Christ, but to have fun at the same time.

Two weeks ago I heard Bill make an announcement: "Yep, a White Elephant party."

"What's that?" Greg questioned.

"You bring a gift, wrapped up. But it's something you don't want. Then we'll exchange them with each other."

Trips to the planitarium, the Six Flags Amusement Park, to cultural events, even visiting with other Christian youth groups. Judi and Bill, along with Harvey (an elder) and Frances, not only the mother of a teen, but a keenly committed mother, keep the youth department exciting and innovative.

Jim Hull works with our youth, too. He's a professional musician in a local supper club. "Cec," he said one day, "I'd like to work with these kids around here. Some musical programs with original arrangements."

"An awful lot of work," one of the adults said.

"We tried a junior choir last year and had limited success," I admitted. "Do you think you could make it work?"

"Sure," he replied. And we'll have a good group. It's really simple."

The three adults standing around glanced at each other. Then Betty broke the silence by laughing. "If you say it's so simple, then do it."

And Jim called for young people with instruments and those who wanted to sing. He organized them for a joint Thanksgiving service when we worshipped with a Lutheran and a Catholic church. Most of the youngsters were frightened and sat in the audience.

Sixth-grade Brian played his French horn, Steve strummed his guitar along with Judi. Four elementary graders and the same number of high-schoolers sang. The children sang a Psalm while the teens did "Day by Day" from *Godspell*. The instruments joined them the second time through.

A newspaper reporter wrote up the service because of its ecumenical nature. She wrote straight reporting on the service with no judgments or evaluations until it came to the youth choir. "The children's choir of Riverdale Presbyterian Church gave a touching rendition of 'Day by Day.' "

Two Sundays later the newly formed choir, now composed of 23 people, sang for the morning service. I saw at least two adults wiping tears from their eyes.

Bobbie, a mother with two school-age children, said, "You don't know how thrilled I felt this morning. We've been in this church eight years. I can't carry a tune but I've wanted to see a youth choir so badly. And this was just beautiful."

One teenager who had been a member of another church and involved in their youth activities said, "This is different. We did things at our other church, but here everyone's so nice to me and—and I like everyone, too!"

\* \* \* \* \* \* \*

There's another area we're learning to think about: the golden age folks.

A year before Pearl died I visited her. She was expecting me and beamed as I walked inside. "See, I even put on a dress today. Just for you."

We laughed together as she said, "First dress I've had on all week. But I had to look my best for you."

"You look great."

"Don't feel good though," she replied as she leaned back in her rocker. A few days earlier she had celebrated her eighty-ninth birthday. "Some days I just don't feel good for anything."

Pearl and her husband, Glenn, were two of the several shut-in members of our church. Even with Pearl gone, Glenn still maintains his own home with the help of a woman who cleans and cooks, and two daughters who live in the city looking in on him daily.

"It's nice that you still think about old-timers like me," Glenn said as he shook my hand.

"Glenn, I don't come by every week, but I don't forget you. I try to come as often as I can."

I meant that. I doubt that Glenn will ever be back in church again. He's ninety and barely gets around. Yet he's still part of our church. I believe it's important to show people like Glenn that we don't write them off. We still care.

"My mother grumbles all the time," a friend said recently. "As long as she was productive, people kept interested in her.

But when she got too feeble to help anyone or to get out to activities, people seemed to cut her off. She went to her church more than sixty years and other than a few of the older ladies who feel as cut off as she does, no one ever calls."

That's happened in a lot of cases—not usually by intention, but rather through neglect or thoughtlessness.

At Riverdale, as I had done in my previous pastorates, I determined to minister to those shut-ins. They're part of our church family. They gave their years of service to the growth of this church. We can't forget them. Their labor and sacrifices made us what we are today.

Bernedine sets up appointments for me on a regular basis, approximately every three weeks. She always calls to make sure they're up to having me drop by, or that they're not going to be at the doctor's. It also gives them a sense of anticipation, something to look forward to. And they seem to have so little to look forward to in their every-day-the-same world.

Second, we record our Sunday worship service. This is especially designed for the shut-ins, although anyone may request the tapes later. When someone convalesces after a lengthy illness, he/she sometimes asks for the tape.

Each Sunday we pray for them by name. I'll usually say, "Now let's pray for our shut-ins. For Leland and Margaret Tarrant . . . for the Oliver Buices . . ."

The journey of the tape recorder and cassette to the shut-ins provides one of the larger forms of our caring ministry to shut-ins. Pauline Hewlett has been the coordinator of this for the past two years. She's been working this through our Sunday school classes.

One August morning she stuck her head into our classroom. "Next month I'd like the Bridge Builders class to take the tape to the shut-ins. Here's a list of their names and addresses. Sign up for one week at a time. In September the Joy class will take the tape."

"I'll do it the first Sunday," Lynn said.

"Give it to me the second," Wanda volunteered.

Polly said, "John and I will take it the last week of the month."

The person responsible takes the tape to the home, staying as short or as long as he/she wants. Sometimes it's a brief, "Hello, I'm Phil and I'll be back Tuesday about four to get the tape."

Or Katy, who sat down and talked for twenty minutes when she took the tape and remained at least that long when she picked it up.

And how do the shut-ins respond?

"That nice Mrs. Steele. She's so friendly. And you know what she did? The next week she brought us a cake she baked. Just for us."

"Mr. Murphey, you see those flowers over there? One of the women's circles brought them for me. They're so pretty. I sit here and keep looking at them over and over. We'll have to throw them away in a couple more days, but they've brought so much pleasure to us."

# 19.
## and a few other things, too

"The other four people sitting with you are your prayer partners. You're going to meet together now for ten minutes. Three other times during this retreat we'll schedule a meeting with your partners. Try to be as free with each other as possible. We don't want to force you to be something you're not. Or to say more than you're ready to say."

After a few more brief statements I said, "For openers, I want each of you to complete this sentence to your partners. 'My greatest spiritual need is...' Then each of you pray for that person before going on to the next one in your group."

That's how I started the activities in our second annual church leaders' retreat. Twenty-three leaders or emerging leaders attended the twenty-hour, overnight retreat at our denominational retreat center.

Among other activities, two outside speakers came. One elder conducted the evening devotional and a second held morning worship. We included a variety of activities such as informal worship, singing, and small-group work, with opportunity for discussion and participation.

An hour-and-a-half before lunch on Saturday morning, I divided them into two groups. "Here are three questions for you to discuss. Elect someone as spokesperson or reporter. Try to limit yourselves to approximately twenty minutes on each question."

I wrote the questions on a large sheet of newsprint.

1. What kind of needs are we *not* meeting at Riverdale Church?
2. What kinds of needs are we meeting effectively?
3. What programs/projects need to be stopped?

For nearly an hour, two independent groups discussed the questions. I walked back and forth, listening but trying not to enter into their conversations.

"How about a continental breakfast before Sunday school? We could serve coffee and donuts on a donation basis."

"Yeah, and juice for the kids."

"Why not a monthly fun night? A time we can get together because we're friends and have fun. It'll also help us know each other better."

Ideas bounced from one individual to another. One person in each group wrote hurriedly to get the ideas on paper.

Later, both groups came together. I had set up a large chalkboard and said, "Now, let's hear your ideas. We'll list them on the board. Don't worry about how impractical they may seem. I'll simply write them down. After they're all on the board, I'll ask for volunteers to investigate the feasibility of integrating the ideas into our church programs."

Ed laughed. "That's what we were all afraid of! Open your mouth and you're a Murphey volunteer!"

"Yeah," Skip replied. "Once I brought up the idea of having a pictoral directory and Cec said, 'Hey, that's a good idea. Why don't you find out the necessary information?' Know what? I ended up being the director of the whole project."

"But you loved it, didn't you?" I laughed back.

Several people teased about being involved.

"But this time it's different," I explained. "We'll write down all the ideas. Some of them can be referred to already existing committees. Those that are left can be handled easily enough. I only want one or two people to explore their feasibility. If you think the idea's workable and will help promote a better organized and more caring congregation, let's find out the way to put it into practice. At that point we'll work toward recruiting someone to head it up."

Several nods.

"Whew," Vickie replied, "I'm glad because I gave four suggestions and I'm not about to take on responsibility for all of them!"

Everyone laughed.

Ben spoke up for his group. "First, we want to give our church a pat on the back. We're not perfect, but we're doing a good job of meeting the needs that we know of."

"That's what our group said, too," Vickie added. "We've grown a lot in our concern about helping people. Especially in the last year or so."

My face beamed. I wanted to stop and hug every one of them. I also wanted to say, "You're coming along. Not always apologizing for imperfections or shortcomings. You've learned to affirm your own achievements and accept affirmation."

I didn't say those words or hug them—not then; that part came later. They were saying "We" and they didn't mean "Cec Murphey's doing a good job." I'm involved and I believe my leadership is crucial. But I'm only one person on the team. They're putting into practice the whole theological concept of priesthood of believers. These leaders are learning to see themselves as ministers. They're voicing needs for specific programs and expressing a willingness to guide projects.

I stopped the flow of conversation long enough to say, "I appreciate you—every one of you. And I thank God for bringing you into our church family. You're the people who make the job of pastor a lot easier."

Then I saw *their* faces beaming.

And why not? We all need appreciation. And that's another area where I'm working.

One day I sat at my desk and leaned back in a reflective mood—my favorite position for that activity. I silently thanked God for the good things happening in our congregation. Immediately several people's names hit my memory line. They had all done so much to help make the church what it is.

*I wonder how often anyone expresses appreciation to them?*

Like Martha. She's doing a great job leading the Women of the Church. They've gotten involved in many projects such as assisting local nursing homes, hospital volunteer programs, sponsoring clinics to check for cancer, as well as many purely religious programs.

Or Ralph. He's put in a lot of time as chairman of our building and grounds committee. Need anything done from repairing a leaky toilet to changing the thermostat control? He's on call and cheerful about it.

I wrote both of them, just to say thanks. I appreciate their commitment. I also wrote three other "Thank-you-for-doing-and-being letters" to folks who've done small but very significant things.

We all need appreciation. Sometimes, I've discovered, simply to say "I've noticed" means a lot. It does to me.

\* \* \* \* \* \* \*

We're re-examining our ideas about recruiting people. I read somewhere that no matter how large a church grows, it maintains a cadre of 45–65 people. They provide the real leadership whether the church has 150 members or 5,000. That fact makes me want to shout, "Being true doesn't mean it has to be true everywhere!"

It's easy enough to realize why most churches or organizations function that way. The same fifty people work hard. They volunteer or get drafted for all the jobs because they show their willingness and aggressiveness in wanting responsibility. Once you start teaching third-graders you either have to go senile in your old age, have a nervous breakdown, or move your membership to another church. Otherwise you're stuck with third-graders the rest of your days.

But does it have to be that way? Is it even healthy?

What of the less reticent members who have abilities, but often are passed over? What about the hidden talents?

I'm pushing committees and program leaders to think seriously about their recruitment every time we start a new phase.

Ask questions like, What kind of leaders do we need? A

teacher? A verbal-oriented individual? One with building skills? An idea person?

They ask, Are there people in the church who might fit that need? Especially people not heavily involved? Don't ask anyone who's already participating in activities. Find uncommitted people or unused talents.

Like Ellen. We knew she worked well with children because she had guided the recreation program two summers in a row for Vacation Bible School. When we formulated plans for our Amuse-You-Tuesday, we called on Ellen. "Interested in giving us a hand?"

Interested? Ellen and Marcia now plan the entire program every month. Then they inform me of my role. "Cec, you tell the story this week." Or, "Can you show us a filmstrip about Noah?"

By contrast there's Vickie. We nearly worked her to her spiritual death when I first came. She, along with Donna and Linda, conducted the worship program for 4 to 5-year-olds during the church hour. Vickie taught kindergarten Sunday school. She set up and coordinated the family night suppers. She was chairperson on a monthly circle meeting. Dinner on the grounds? Call Vickie. Decorations for a party? Oh, Vickie's so talented. We even elected her an elder in 1976.

That's not fair. Not to Vickie, certainly. But not fair to at least seven other people in the church! Those others could have taken over those forms of ministry. Beginning in early 1976 we started changing that. Nancy's in charge of the 4 to 5-year-old worship. Barry and Denise teach the kindergarten Sunday school. A different Nancy, along with Beckye, set up and prepare for family night suppers. Rita now chairs the circle Vickie attends. Vickie's still an elder. She has enough responsibility in other areas to keep her busy, involved, and interested—but not overworked. We care about Vickie.

Volunteers need breathing spaces, time to drop out of the game for an inning, the opportunity to say, "My interests have changed and now I'd like to get involved in . . ."

So my first suggestion to all committees and project leaders is, *let's look for someone not already involved.* What kind of talent do unrecognized members have that can be utilized?

Second, *let people know what they're volunteering for (as specifically as possible). Also let them know how important the task is.*

"Oh, anyone can keep the nursery," I heard one woman tell another. "For an hour you can put up with anything."

Why not try a different approach. How about the conversation I overheard? Estelle said, "You know, that nursery is a wonderful idea. It gives couples with babies a chance to get away from the crying and just enjoy being together. And neither has to jump to feed the baby or change a diaper."

Third, *make it clear how long they're expected to work.*

For instance, one day I said, "David, I'd like you to teach a young adults' class for three months. That's all I'm asking. Try it. If you don't feel comfortable at the end of that time, I'll take it over again."

David had gone through a teacher-training program, possessed a sharp mind, and a good biblical background. He agreed to teach. At the end of the three months David said, "I'm giving up the class. It's just not the right age group for me."

I released David. Six months later he became co-teacher of a different Sunday school class.

* * * * * * *

*Caring. Freedom.* These two words pin down the area of struggle in my life and in my Christian ministry.

Caring stands at the head of the list. That's largely what I've been describing in this book. My own growth in learning to care, as well as that of members of our congregation.

As we care, we accept that people also need the right to be free. To back off. To reject. To remain indifferent. To say no. Sometimes we find that difficult to understand, but we try to hear what they're saying.

Charlie joined our church three months ago. He's one of those quiet but committed men who's always willing to help in any way needed. I told him one evening how much I had learned to appreciate him.

He smiled shyly and said, "You know why we picked this church? Because you didn't push. You let us know that you were interested in us, but you didn't make us feel guilty for not coming, or make us feel like sinners because we hadn't already joined a church."

Charlie said what I believe has been happening in many lives. People sense they're cared about. And they respond to that caring.

Charlie is head usher for our early service. He's always there and I know everything's going to be ready for worship—from lights on to bulletins in the narthex.

\* \* \* \* \* \* \*

The other night, one of the elders said to me, "You're happy here, aren't you? You're not planning to move to another church?"

"I'm happier here than I've ever been anywhere except . . ." and then I stopped. Shirley and I had been missionaries nearly six years in Kenya, East Africa. Although we had gone through a lot of hardships and struggles,[1] it had always remained the highpoint in my life. But as I started to add "except for my years in Africa," I stopped.

*That's no longer true.*

Riverdale is special—the most special place I've lived all my life. Perhaps part of it is because I'm away from Kenya. Perhaps part of it is my maturing and living in the present. But largely it's because I'm experiencing vital, exciting, caring Christianity in greater depth than I ever have before.

I chuckled. "Strange, I was going to say except Africa, but I realize I'm happier here than anyplace I've ever been. And no, I'm not planning to move on. Did I make you think I was?"

"I wondered. Nothing you did or said. It's just that I've been around the church awhile. Whenever a pastor gets things going

---

1. I've told this story in my book, *But God Has Promised*, Creation House, 1976.

in a church and moving ahead, then he starts looking for a church that's bigger and—"

\* \* \* \* \* \* \*

"At this moment, I'm willing to stay at Riverdale Presbyterian Church the rest of my active ministry. I've already made a commitment to the Lord of my willingness."

He seemed satisfied.

"I don't know what the future holds, but for the moment . . ."

That elder made a significant gesture: he hugged me.

He cared about me; I cared about him. His physical movement helped me to see that many of our folks had moved beyond theological discussions and objective Bible studies. The human ingredient had added life to truths we had known all along. That simple gesture spoke for the whole congregation. One individual reaching out toward another—that's living theology.

*You set the example, Lord, because you bridged the gap. You loved . . . You gave. We're still learning how to respond.*

# 20.
## my motives are showing

"Of course, I don't want to steal you away from your own church. Not if you're really happy there. *And* if you're being ministered to," he added with a wide grin, showing his large teeth and distinct overbite. "We have a wonderful congregation. So many activities to offer at Grace Church . . ."

He let the sentence hang unfinished.

"We like our own church," I admitted, "And we're really not interested—"

"I hope there's solid preaching going on where you attend. And real dynamic prayer warriors at work."

I nodded.

"At our church," he continued, "people love one another. But we've also got one of the best outreach programs in the county. We have the best trained Sunday school teachers you can find anywhere. Seventy-eight per cent of them are actually teachers by profession. Our adult classes are growing all the time—in fact, we started two new classes only last year. You ought to visit our children's activities—we have programs going on four nights a week for kids. And . . ." he paused and smiled again. "Of course, like I said, I'm not trying to steal you from your own church."

I wondered if he knew how hard he was attempting to manipulate me. I resented the heavy-handed sales pitch. He sounded very much like a man who once tried to convince my mother she needed a vacuum cleaner. Even after she explained she didn't need one, he kept pushing for a sale. He stayed nearly two hours and all he got for his labors was a glass of iced tea.

The experience with the member of Grace Church happened to me long before I went into the ministry. I've met his type many times.

There are a few more subtle ones.

Like preacher Hershel. He knew which church I belonged to, but he nearly always said, "If you ever decide you want to attend a really good church, come on over." Because he smiled I wasn't supposed to take offence. But his eyes told me he was throwing out the line, hoping to hook me.

The methods vary; the attitudes don't. They're always throwing out the hook.

I realized I wrote *they* above. My methods may not have been quite so transparent, but I've often discovered myself doing the same kinds of things. I want to see a growing church. That means an enlarging membership. Increased resources. Additional talent coming to the fore.

It's happening. Each year we are increasing our membership. However, that very desire for increase creates a subtle trap for success-oriented types like myself.

I used to tag everyone I met as a potential member for our church. Give them the sales message. Hit heavy on the kinds of programs that appeal. How could they *not* want to have fellowship with us? We have so much to offer.

This isn't a chapter on how I overcame selfish motives and can now leave it all to the Holy Spirit. I still want new people in our congregation. I'm more honest in my approach. My motives shine with a little more integrity.

Two experiences happened in the summer of 1976 that helped me greatly. I met Charlie and Irene at a community-type fellowship meeting. They lived in our general area and began visiting us regularly.

I went to their house one evening and chatted with them. They were looking for a church home, both had taught Sunday school and especially wanted to work with pre-teens. Both read music, sang, and had always been active in choir. They seemed like an ideal catch for our church.

"But you see," Irene said, "we're not sure about where to join. We like you and the people are friendly enough...."

"We want a church with a little more activity," Charlie said. "You're just really getting started in your programs. We want God's will, but..."

I told them of the opportunities for service and for growth. The challenges we saw. Then I said, "Look, I want God's will for you folks, too. Let's make a prayer covenant together. Let's pray every day for the will of God in your lives. I promise to pray until I hear from you of your decision."

We agreed and sealed the covenant with prayer.

I continued to fulfill my promise. "Lord, you know how much they have to offer. Bring them to us." I was already mentally ticking off things they could do. We had so many uses for their talents.

But they never joined our church. In fact, I never saw them again. After three months I called them on the phone. "Oh, we decided to join another church. It's so much bigger and we really like larger churches."

Shortly afterwards Gene and Thelma visited us and I went to their home. They were also praying about which church to join.

Thelma and Gene said quite frankly, "There's another church we've been visiting. We like it but for different reasons than we like Riverdale. We just don't know what the Lord wants us to do at present."

I entered into a prayer contract with them. We would pray separately every day until they felt the Lord had given them an answer. Two weeks later Gene called. "Thought you'd like to know that Thelma and I have made up our minds."

"Gene, that's great that you've settled the issue. I'm sure you'll be happy in your new church."

"We feel we've found the place where the Lord wants us."

"That's important," I replied, assuming they had decided on the other church they had mentioned.

"We've been visiting around several months. But the more we pray, the more we sense God's direction for us."

"Gene, I appreciate your calling to tell me. We've fulfilled our contract together." I started to hang up.

"Oh, by the way, it's Riverdale Presbyterian that we're going to join."

\* \* \* \* \* \* \*

Dealing with those families helped me in sorting out this question of motive. I wanted both couples to join our church—and I knew both had talents to offer. But I prayed differently in each instance.

For Charlie and Irene, I had prayed, "Send them where you want them. But, Lord, let it be to our church." For Gene and Thelma—and perhaps because I was nearly convinced they would go elsewhere—I prayed quite objectively, "Lord, we all want your will in the matter."

That double incident caused me to do a lot of soul searching about my motives in dealing with people. They still aren't always perfect and I live with that. But I keep trying.

I've learned the hard way never to count heads in advance. Take the Goldman family for instance. We first met when they started going through a long siege of sickness. We helped Seth find a new job, shared groceries with them from our food pantry, and twice picked up the children for Sunday school when both Seth and Martha were sick.

Then Seth received a promotion and they never came back to our church. One member grumbled, "All that effort and then . . ."

I'm sure I had thought the same thing several times myself. But I answered him and realized my words were true. "Did we do it to help them or to get them into our church? I wonder if we did it out of love or to make them feel as though they owed us something?"

"Yeah, you're right."

And I knew I was. If we gave freely—openly and out of concern for them as people—then we had no strings attached.

And my understanding of real love is just that: no strings. We help because we care, because we want to see people happy. They owe us nothing.

If they then turn around and join our fellowship, we've gained. But they have no obligation to us.

Sid and Eve, members of another church, needed help. Sid and Eve were unhappy in their own church, but we did nothing to encourage them to leave.

We paid one-half of their month's rent and presented them with two large boxes of groceries. The next time I saw Sid he thanked me profusely. "We're going to visit your church next week."

"Hey, wait a minute. You're welcome—we'd love to have you come. But our giving you help had nothing to do with your membership. We did it because we wanted to help. That's all. Honest. No other motive." And again, as I said the words, I felt my answer was true.

"Fine. But we can come anyway, can't we?"

And they did.

I still battle the question of motives. I want my intentions to be pure. Realistically, I know they're often mixed. But the Lord's working with me to get this all sorted out.

I've set up a few guidelines for myself which help me in this area. *First,* I quote to myself frequently:

> *The heart is deceitful above all things,*
>   *and desperately corrupt;*
> *who can understand it?*
>                     *(Jeremiah 17:9)*

That means my heart, too!

Even when I think I've been honest, I'm not always sure. In our culture, we're taught to say the right things to win the other person. To satisfy his or her questions. To dodge issues. In short, to manipulate the person into liking us, and then we can present our product. That means we often give a false impression of what we're really like. We don't lie—we only make everything sound a little more grand than it perhaps is.

*Second,* I pray for the Lord to search my heart. "God, help me. Don't let me push. Don't let me start a subtle sales campaign and manipulate people. Help me talk to these folks and when I leave to feel that I've conducted myself with integrity."

I felt good recently after visiting Roger and Debbie. They had been referred to me as prospects. I had visited them, they came to our church once, and then I went back. We talked for 45 minutes. Roger said, "I'm searching. I want to find God's will in all of this and go to the right church. I'm just not sure where it is. We've been visiting around."

I said, "Fine. I've told you about us. I won't be back again unless you invite me. I'd love to have you become a part of our fellowship but I won't push you."

After leaving their house, I sat inside my Dodge Colt. No decisions or commitments made by Roger and Debbie, but I felt a sense of peace within myself. Before starting the engine I prayed, "Lord, you love this young couple. You have a church home where they can be happy and useful. Guide them."

Did they visit us again? No, in fact they joined a local Baptist church. They're both active and Roger's becoming involved as an usher.

*Third,* everyone isn't going to respond. I'm learning to live with the reality that all people don't view me as the best pastor/preacher/teacher since the death of the Apostle Paul. They don't see our church as the most loving/affirming/caring congregation of people in the world. And it's not our responsibility to convince them!

We're learning to do what we can and then allow the Holy Spirit an opportunity to bring in those he wants as part of our fellowship.

Two years ago I first met William and Suzannah. Deep inside I knew they wouldn't fit into our church. It's easy to say William was stuffy and anti-social. Or that Suzannah hardly knew how to say a kind word about anyone. Both are highly educated and both are living by much higher standards than our predominately middle class church. But they were human beings—live and breathing.

I went after them, cultivated their friendship. Eventually they joined our church. The few activities they did become involved in, they offended people. After less than a year, William angrily stormed out of one of our activities and yelled, "You're the most stupid, closed-minded people I've ever met."

We never brought about a reconciliation. And had I allowed the Holy Spirit originally to guide my efforts . . . ? I can only guess what the results might have been.

In this whole area of learning to care, motives have a lot to do with it. True caring for people lifts us above personal gain or numerical growth.

Becoming more sensitive to my motives doesn't mean lack of interest in reaching people. I still want an increase in fellowship. I still invite people as freely as ever. We can offer them help. New hope. A sense of being cared about.

And I'm struggling so that I can always pray (and mean):

> *Search me, O God, and know my heart!*
> *Try me and know my thoughts!*
> *And see if there be any wicked way in me,*
> *and lead me in the way everlasting!*
> (Psalm 139:23–24)

# p. s.

By the time you read this, Riverdale Presbyterian Church will no longer be the same church it was when I wrote about it. We're changing. Any living, growing organization keeps changing. And my hope is that we'll always be asking, "What kinds of needs are we not meeting?"

"What can we do about—?"

I wrote this book as a *guide,* not as a *model.* You can find all kinds of imperfections around here. But I hope it will stimulate you to look at your own local church and ask, "Lord, what do YOU want to happen here?" Your church will turn out differently than ours.

And isn't that exciting? Like snowflakes, no two alike!

What's happening in your church? I'd love to hear from you. I warn you, however, that if you send along an idea, it might click with me. Then, we'd incorporate it or modify it in our congregation. That's part of the growing process.

If you'd like to share what's happening in your church, write me either in care of the publisher or at Box 208, Riverdale, Georgia 30274.